D0463764

A BOOK OF MEDITATIONS

THREADS OF
PARADISE

Other books by Christopher de Vinck

The Power of the Powerless
Only the Heart Knows How to Find Them
Augusta and Trab
Songs of Innocence and Experience
Simple Wonders

A BOOK OF MEDITATIONS

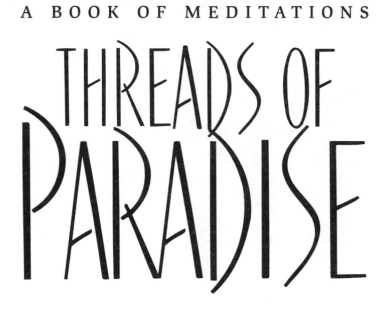

THREADS OF PARADISE

IN THE FABRIC OF EVERYDAY LIFE

CHRISTOPHER DE VINCK

ZondervanPublishingHouse
Grand Rapids, Michigan

A Division of HarperCollins*Publishers*

Threads of Paradise
Copyright © 1996 by Christopher de Vinck

Requests for information should be addressed to:

🏭 ZondervanPublishingHouse
Grand Rapids, Michigan 49530

Library of Congress Cataloging-in-Publication Data
De Vinck, Christopher, 1951–
   Threads of paradise : in the fabric of everyday life / Christopher de Vinck
    p. cm.
   ISBN: 0–310–49931–3 (hardcover : alk. paper)
   1. Christian life—Meditations. I. Title.
BV4501.2.D494   1996
242—dc20   95-25256
                                                   CIP

This edition printed on acid-free paper and meets the American National Standards Institute Z39.48 standard.

All Scripture quotations, unless otherwise indicated, are taken from the *Holy Bible: New International Version*®. NIV®. Copyright © 1973, 1978, 1984 by International Bible Society. Used by permission of Zondervan Publishing House. All rights reserved.

Edited by Mary McCormick and John Sloan
Interior design by Sue Koppenol

Printed in the United States of America

96 97 98 99 00 01 02 /❖ DC/ 10 9 8 7 6 5 4 3 2 1

For Fr. John Catoir

Contents

Introduction

Many years ago when I was a child, I was given a cricket cage. Inside the cage sat a small bamboo cricket. The legs were made of two thin strands of bamboo. I carried the cage with me during my walks into the garden.

"Sing, cricket," I'd say. Then I would listen, and there was singing. My cricket sang cowboy songs, Disney songs, French songs. I was always impressed by how well my cricket sang and how much it sounded like my own voice.

At times, if the cricket behaved, I pulled up the little door and shook the cricket onto my hand. It never jumped away.

One afternoon I allowed the cricket to sit on a rock beside the small pond my father had built at the mouth of a stream that flowed through the garden. What I liked best about the stream was the six-inch-high waterfall. There was just enough water and fall that in the middle of the night I could hear the water spilling onto itself in a rolling, boiling, churning sound—the sound of melancholy—though ten-year-old boys ought not know melancholy. I simply curled under my blanket, and listened through my open window to the passing water that continued on its way along the pebbles and sand.

The afternoon I am telling you about was an ordinary afternoon. The ripest raspberries had been eaten for the day. The catbird had already established her domain off to the right in the mock orange bush. My father was painting the mast of a sailboat he had built in the

11

basement. My mother was typing. My brothers and sisters were making grass huts.

I found a small, plastic boat that I was using to catch lizards. The pond was still. Sometimes there was a crayfish or a frog, but there were always lizards crawling at the bottom. The great fun was to see how many I could catch. I was about to break my record, twelve, when my brother shouted, "Chrissy! Come on and try our hut!"

Sure enough, in the middle of the lawn stood what looked like a haystack. My sister and brother had been able to construct a rough frame with rope and sticks, then they laced the recently cut and dried lawn grass into the frame.

"Come on, Chrissy," my brother waved as he disappeared around the opposite side of the construction.

I ran up the lawn and looked into the hut's door. There, like two chickens curled in a egg, sat Anne and Bruno.

"Come on in, Chrissy," Anne said. "There's plenty of room."

I crawled in and squeezed between my sister and brother. Then Bruno began to tickle me. I tried to tickle him back, but then Anne started tickling me, so I tried to sock her in the nose, but then Bruno came to my defense and began tickling Anne. She wanted to sock us both in the nose, but then she and I began tickling Bruno. Then we all laughed and fell backward at the same time. We tumbled through the grass wall, and the hut collapsed around us.

"Dinner!" My mother called from the back porch. "Dinner."

My father stopped painting. We quickly brushed the grass from our clothes until Anne grabbed a clump and threw it at Bruno's head. Then he picked up a clump of grass and began chasing Anne. I tried to keep up with the two of them as they climbed up the rock walls and ran toward the house.

By the time we sat down at the dinner table, we all looked like the scarecrow from *The Wizard of Oz*. We said grace, ate our meal, washed the dishes, played Monopoly, and went to bed. Another day. Another adventure. I undressed, opened my window, and curled under my blanket. Then I heard the peaceful, falling water from the stream, and that is when I remembered—"My cricket."

I had never before gone out of the house on my own in the dark. For some reason I didn't want to tell anyone about my abandoned cricket. I dressed, crept down the backstairs and out into the yard.

A few hours earlier, all was green and yellow and blue. In the dark, all was shadows and mystery and fear.

I jumped over the rock wall onto the lawn. The mound of grass that was the hut looked like a sleeping lion. The raspberry bushes looked like miniature elephants. I walked upon the evening dew, smelled the coldness, heard the distant dog barking. The house leaned against me with wide, bright eyes. Often it is the scenery and not the story that wins our attention.

I knew that I was a ten-year-old boy who needed friends, who believed in singing crickets, who lived a life squeezed between older and younger brothers and sisters. I know now that I was a child placed in the protection of my mother and father, and all that I learned about peace and nature and the size of the moon I learned in the backyard.

When I reached the rock where I had left my bamboo cricket, I was startled. No cricket. *Perhaps,* I thought, *it was the wrong rock.* But, no. I found the empty little boat I used to catch the lizards, which was beside the only rock of that size, my cricket's rock. I felt in the darkness around the base of the rock, but no cricket. I did find the cage, but that was empty.

When I began to notice that the lights in the house were being extinguished, I grabbed the cage and ran back over the lawn, past the pile of grass, over the rock wall, and back up the porch stairs.

By the time I crept into my room and curled back into bed, the house was still. The distant stream churned and rolled and churned and rolled as I mourned the loss of my bamboo cricket.

I never found the cricket and have come to believe it joined the other crickets in the summer symphony. To this day one of my favorite sounds is the sound of the crickets at night as they *crick-crack* and twiddle and scratch into the deep night as I sleep, and I often think about my bamboo cricket, free from its cage.

We all break out eventually. My sister and brother and I rolled out of the grass hut, laughing. The cricket, too, is laughing on its way, like the water that still rolls through my father's garden, going somewhere, freeing itself up.

My father gave up sailing many years ago, but he has, framed on his wall in his bedroom, the blueprints of that boat he built when he was a young man.

I hope that this book will help you understand from where you have come and to where you can go: a place where the yard is green and blue and yellow, where the water runs through, and the bamboo cricket sings—better known as God's place, the eternal home with the Father.

Everyone who drinks this water will be thirsty again, but whoever drinks the water I give him will never thirst. Indeed, the water I give him will become in him a spring of water welling up to eternal life.

JOHN 4:13–14

We Are Strong
in the Eyes of the Lord

The blind receive sight, the lame walk, those who have leprosy are cured, the deaf hear, the dead are raised, and the good news is preached to the poor. Blessed is the man who does not fall away on account of me.

LUKE 7:22–23

This past winter my wife and I visited friends just outside of Manchester, Vermont. We arrived late on a Friday evening, tired and hungry. Our friends greeted us warmly, fed us soup and delicious bread, then we walked over to the fireplace and sat peacefully on the couch.

We began talking about the weekend, the different things we might like to do. "Lots of antique stores," Ellen suggested. "You could just spend the day hiking," Jerry added. Our host and hostess suggested good restaurants, the best skiing, "and you could visit Weston," Ellen remembered. "They have a terrific general store with everything you can imagine."

"Weston?" I asked. "How far are we from Weston?"

"Oh, only fifteen or twenty minutes."

How could I not have realized that we were so close to Weston? I was a bit puzzled, although I should have known. Weston. I hadn't been to Weston, Vermont, in fifteen years—since the Benedictine monks buried my brother Oliver in the Priory's cemetery just beyond the pond over a small hill.

"I'd like to go to Weston."

The next morning Roe, our friend Ellen, and I drove through the winding roads of middle Vermont at the foot of the mountains. We passed quick-moving streams with loaves of snow risen on opposite banks, and a man on a sleigh being pulled by a brown workhorse. Smoke bloomed from a distant chimney. Vermont. All that we imagined it to be, all that we pretend it is: maple syrup, pine trees, steeples watching over us.

After our short drive, after browsing in the Weston General Store, we continued our trip to the Priory.

When we pulled in the driveway and drove past the parking lot, I realized that the monks were probably gone, on their winter retreat. I was right. We spoke with a kind woman in the bookstore, sat in the chapel for a moment, then I said, "I'd like to go to Oliver's grave."

Roe and Ellen walked to the parking lot to fetch the car while I turned left after we walked from the chapel. I jumped a small fence and began to run across a field of white snow.

No one, obviously, had crossed this field since the most recent storm. My boots broke the silence as I stepped into the snow. *Crunch. Crunch. Crunch.* I had fed Oliver his dinner since I was eight years old. *Crunch. Crunch. Crunch.* Oliver was blind. *Crunch.* Oliver was crippled. *Crunch.* Oliver sustained severe brain damage before birth. *Crunch. Crunch. Crunch.* Oliver lived in my parents' home for thirty-two years. *Crunch. Crunch.* I hadn't been to Oliver's grave since his funeral in the spring of 1980.

I stopped running toward the cemetery for a moment. I turned around to check on Roe and Ellen. Roe had driven the car to the far side of the field and waited. Obviously they had decided not to walk through the deep snow to join me.

I turned and began to run again. I felt so alone. Running. Running. Past the pond. Running. Up the small hill. I stood still on the top of the hill and looked down into the cemetery. I had forgotten, of course, that the flat tombstones would be covered with snow. I turned and waved to Roe and Ellen. Roe beeped the car horn as I disappeared down the side of the hill and into the cemetery.

The only thing Oliver could do for thirty-two years was laugh. He could not speak. He never cried.

The closer I approached the gravesite, the more I noticed small indentations in the snow. Then I realized that in each spot where there was a tombstone, there was a small depression in the snow. There are perhaps thirty or forty graves in the little cemetery.

I leaned over and brushed the snow from a grave in about the spot where I thought Oliver was buried. Wrong name. *Oliver liked ice cream.*

I stepped down the line and brushed the snow from the next stone. Wrong name. *Oliver had convulsions about once a month.*

I stepped down the line and brushed the snow from the next stone. *Wrong name. Oliver died in his mother's arms.*

I stepped down the line and brushed the snow from the next stone.

Oliver de Vinck
April 22, 1948—March 12, 1980
Blessed are the pure in heart for they shall see God.

And I cried in the snow. And I wanted to be eight years old again, carrying Oliver's dinner bowl up to him. I pressed my hand on his tombstone and remembered what my mother always said to me:

"Oliver will be waiting for you in heaven. He will run to you, embrace you, and say, 'Thank you, Christopher, for feeding me all those delicious dinners.'"

I stood up, brushed the snow from my knees, and began to run. I ran back up the little hill. I ran down the other side. I ran back across the open field, waving my arms to Roe and Ellen.

When John the Baptist sent two messengers to Jesus to ask if He is, indeed, the Messiah, Jesus said, *"Go back and report to John what you have seen and heard: The blind receive sight, the lame walk, those who have leprosy are cured, the deaf hear, the dead are raised, and the good news is preached to the poor. Blessed is the man who does not fall away on account of me"* (Luke 7: 22–23).

My mother was the messenger when I was a child. She told me what Jesus said. Oliver will receive sight. Oliver will walk. Oliver will hear. Oliver will be risen from the dead. Lord, how I look forward to that dance and jig with my brother at the gates of paradise.

Look for the weak people in your life today, and see if you can discover what makes them strong, for then you will understand God's power.

Foolish are the people who believe they are powerful, for they do not know the power of the Lord Jesus Christ: His power of love, His power of eternal life, His power of forgiveness, His power of compassion, His power of grace, His power of the Holy Spirit.

What Is Your Name?

What is your name, so that we may honor you when your word comes true?

JUDGES 13:17

I heard a story about Berry. I do not know why she was called Berry, but this is what I heard about her. She was born in a trailer in South Dakota. Her father was a locksmith, and her mother worked in the post office.

After a terrible fire in the trailer, both the father and mother perished. Berry sustained burns over eighty percent of her body, was blinded for life, and became morose and unhappy.

Berry never married. She attended school up to the tenth grade, then she was taken north by her aunt, who had a flower business in New York State.

Berry spent many days in the florist shop, answering phones and dictating orders on a tape recorder that her aunt played back whenever she was able to catch up on business.

The children in the neighborhood teased Berry by calling her names such as "Alligator Lady," or "Goofy Eyes." At first these things hurt the young woman; then, one day, Berry just laughed and asked the children what their names were.

The local children soon became enchanted with this Miss Berry who laughed and knew the smell of every flower they brought her.

One boy, who was particularly shy, fetched Miss Berry's mail each day and read it to her.

Miss Berry learned braille, wrote letters to the newspaper about the pollution she smelled while sitting out back where the maple tree grew. And to the boy who brought the mail she began to read stories about pirates, airplanes, and secret spies who rescued people from terrible fates by hiding them in the mountains of Europe.

Miss Berry stayed with her aunt until the aunt died. She attended college, received her degree in law, and became a public defender for abused children.

When Miss Berry died, she had no family. A young man from the old neighborhood read in the papers that Miss Berry had died, so he went over and said that he would like to make a contribution.

Before she died, the only thing that Miss Berry didn't tend to herself was a headstone, so the young man paid for the headstone. When he was asked what he would like to have engraved on the stone, he thought for some time, then wrote a few words on a piece of paper and handed it to the stonecutter.

The stonecutter read the words and smiled. "I also knew her. These words will suit her just fine: MISS BERRY: SHE LOVED ALL THE FLOWERS AND ALL THE CHILDREN.

When we human beings are confronted with something we do not understand, we become suspicious, just as the children were when they first met Miss Berry. We need to have answers. We need to know. And if we do not understand something, as the children didn't at first understand Miss Berry, we become afraid, or we make jokes, or we push for answers.

During the time of Christ, people were puzzled about a man who was baptizing. They wanted to know if he was Jesus. John the Baptist *confessed freely, "I am not the Christ."*

They asked him, "Then who are you? Are you Elijah?"

He said, "I am not."

"Are you the Prophet?"

He answered, "No."

Finally they said, "Who are you? Give us an answer to take back to those who sent us. What do you say about yourself?"

John replied in the words of Isaiah the prophet, "I am the voice of one calling in the desert, 'Make straight the way for the Lord'" (John 1:20–23).

One of the most significant things we can do is answer to God, "What do you say about yourself?"

I think Miss Berry would simply laugh and say, "Well, the children called me Alligator Woman; I became a lawyer; I like flowers; and there was a boy who read my mail to me each day for eight years. I learned to read because of him."

Who we are is connected to those we love and to those who have influenced us toward goodness. John the Baptist loved Jesus and was influenced by His words. John was never the same because of Christ's spiritual intervention.

The small boy who read to Miss Berry intervened in her spirit, and she was no longer the same person because of the child's kindness.

We all have the potential to be the one who baptizes. We all have the potential to be moved to action. Today let us make straight the way for the Lord.

I am Your child, Lord. You have given me Your name, the name of God blessed upon my forehead with water. Thank You, Lord, for making me in Your image. Thank You for the confidence of who I am.

The Fate of a Harsh Man

The LORD works righteousness and justice for all the oppressed.
PSALM 103:6

I heard a story once about the ant and the baker. It seems that there was an ant that lived under the baker's house. The baker lived on the second floor with his son. The baker's shop was on the first floor, with the window facing the main street of town.

Everyone believed the baker to be a man of honor and humor. His only visible fault was his harsh manner toward his son.

Whenever a customer entered the shop, the baker would wipe his hands and stand on the opposite side of the counter and wait for an order. The bigger the order, the better the service. The baker would extend his hand across the counter and grasp the eager customer's hand and shake it, vigorously shouting at the same time to his son, "Check the oven, fool, and find the most freshly baked loaves for our kind customer."

The son would step back to the oven, press the wooden pallet into the oven's mouth, and sift around for the best loaf of bread that was ready to be sold.

Those who came to the bakery with small orders received older bread, and the son received harsher treatment.

One afternoon the ant entered the bakery for the first time. When the baker stepped up to the counter, he wiped his hands, looked around, and saw no one, although he was certain that he had heard the door swing open. "Imbecile!" the baker called out to his son. "Why have you left the door open?"

"I have not been near the door, Father," the boy answered meekly.

The father looked around, but he did not notice the ant on the floor. "Get back to work," the father yelled.

The ant edged around the corner and whispered to the boy, "Psssst."

The boy looked down from his work and saw the ant. "Yes?" asked the boy.

"Do you have some crumbs for sale?" asked the ant.

The boy looked up at his father, who was busy combing his hair, then he turned to the ant and said, "I do not believe we have a crumb so big that we would have to charge you."

"Oh, no," said the ant. "A labor made is traded for a labor made. I will give you a pound of gold for your bread."

"But," said the boy, "no crumb is worth that much. Here. Take what you need."

The ant said to the boy, "Because of your kindness I will triple my pay for your bread: three bags of gold."

"But," said the boy, "that is a king's price for such a small favor. Please. Let me give you a whole loaf of our finest bread. This will last you all winter and beyond."

The ant was about to offer the boy a hundred bags of gold when the father stepped on the ant, twisted his shoe against the floor, and struck the boy on the back of the head. "Fool! Wasting your time fiddling with useless ants. Return to your work."

Within a year the colony of hungry ants ate the foundation of the bakery. The building was condemned. The bakery was torn down, the baker died of the gout, and the son became a carpenter and prospered.

We have all been victims of harsh people in one way or another: an angry boss, a disgruntled neighbor, an angry father or mother. Often we try to deflect the pain that is hurled in our direction. Often we try to send the pain back in defense.

Perhaps someone has hurt you recently. Try to figure out why people are the way they are. Perhaps you could write the person a letter of peace and forgiveness. If that person does not have the wisdom to offer peace, nor the humility to accept forgiveness, step away from that person and pray that his or her foundation does not crumble away.

Merciful Lord, my protector, merciful Savior, grant me patience with those who persecute me; grant me strength to endure their hurtful ways against me. I follow in Your footsteps to the cross with faith, with trust, with gratitude for Your presence, merciful Lord, wise Lord, Lord of comfort, Lord of peace.

The Child of Light

And a voice from heaven said, "This is my Son, whom I love; with him I am well pleased."

MATTHEW 3:17

It is difficult to imagine what it must have been like for Mary when she gave birth to her Son, Jesus. She knew that this child was her Son, but she also knew that she not only carried the child but also the world, the world's future, the world's hope.

When my first son was born, my father looked through the nursery window and announced, "Yes! It is a baby!" I enjoyed my father's straightforward humor. I also enjoyed looking through the glass. There he was—David, my first son. I knew from the first moment of his life that my life and the life of my wife, Roe, would be changed forever. Children force us to look at the world differently. They remind us that there is something called life and mystery and hope.

The day we brought David home from the hospital, it snowed and snowed. I remember that the trees were bent low like ballet dancers at the end of a performance. The air was cold. The house stood at the end of the front walk waiting for us. The house was soon to be a new house, a house of the child.

When we stepped inside and closed the door, after we pulled off our coats, placed the baby's things on the floor, Roe placed David in my arms. I walked to the window and held him in the fresh afternoon light.

I looked and looked at my son's eyes, at his face, at his small hands. I felt like saying, "So, where did you come from?" I felt like asking, "What message do you have to tell us?"

The doorbell rang. It was our neighbor Janet, who rushed over to see the baby. "He looks so much like you, Chris," she said. Roe laughed, saying "Poor kid." I laughed and said "Lucky boy, handsome as his father."

Roe and Janet walked around the neighborhood. I was alone in the house with the boy, the star, the moment of wonder, the future president of the United States, my son, my child.

I am pierced with the passing of time, the lost images that cannot be retrieved. Children grow up so fast. How many times have we said this to ourselves? My son David is a teenager. Soon he will be a man. I see his smile. I recognize his voice. He is still my child, and I am proud of his work.

The sun follows the moon, and the moon disappears into the sunlight once again. Day after day and night after night we march in step with our responsibilities, with our joys and sorrows. I watch my son walk out of the house each morning and watch him walk down the street toward school. Sometimes he remembers to turn around and wave.

Because of my son, I discovered a part of myself. Roe and I have three children today who have given us triple joy, triple peace. It is in the voice of our children that we can hear whispers of ourselves and the language of innocence.

I can easily imagine Mary holding her Son near a window as the sunlight bathed them both. It is the same sun that places its warmth against our skin. We are placed in the light. Children understand this light.

Our children need us no matter what age they are. Reach out to your children today in a way that is significant. Perhaps call them at work, or leave a message, or send them flowers, or invite them out to lunch. You will see them in a familiar light.

I never forget to wave to my son even if he doesn't turn around as he walks down the street toward his new day.

Praise the Lord, for He is the Son. Hallelujah! Hallelujah! All hail and praise to the Son of God. I come to praise the Lord.

Beauty Breeds Beauty

But now you must rid yourself of all such things as these: anger,
rage, malice, slander, and filthy language from your lips.
COLOSSIANS 3:8

I was brought up in the shadows of American poetry. I was
brought up with the notion that words are beautiful things.

When those things we loved as children are threatened, we tend
to be defensive and a bit disappointed that the world does, indeed,
weigh heavily against all that is good and beautiful and innocent.

Day after day, as I sit in my little office across from the library in the
high school where I work as an administrator, I listen as many young
people walk through the hallways on the way to their next class. I listen
with envy because I miss teaching. As the district's new language arts
supervisor, I no longer teach. I was a teacher for the past seventeen
years, and suddenly I find myself cut away from the daily dialogue with
young people in my classroom, so I listen as the teenagers pass my
office, and I smile at what I hear: concerns about grades, the interest in
the spring play, the goings-on with parents, girlfriends, schoolwork. I
catch only bits and pieces because there is a constant stream of young
people walking by my office.

I take great delight in hearing their voices. The sounds of
teenagers' voices passing in the hallway are among my most favorite
sounds, which include the trains roaring through the night, the

crickets in the summer, the sounds of my own children playing in the neighborhood, the music of Aaron Copland, and my mother's voice with her Belgian accent.

But there is also a sadness connected with my eavesdropping. We human beings have a terrible habit of turning beauty into ugliness. I think this is true with sexuality, art, radio, television, clothes, books, the environment, friendships. Everywhere in our lives we see things that chip away at beauty bit by bit.

When I listen to the sounds of those bright, healthy, strong, beautiful voices passing in the hallway, I am truly charmed and delighted, but then time and time again I hear the "F" word or the "S" word, some ugly word peppered in the dialogue that turns the songs of youth into the voices of tired, clichéd, vulgar old men and women.

The use of vulgar language chips away at beauty. Ugliness spreading throughout a conversation destroys the beauty of the language. Speaking vulgar words is like wearing ugly clothes to school.

I realize that crass language is the language of camaraderie, the language of the "hip," the language of the cool, the language of the adult world behind closed doors. Vulgarity is the language of the college dorm, the backrooms, the dugout, the bar, the party, and the high school hallway. We human beings have a funny notion that swearing is sophisticated. I believe we all want to be different. We all want to be looked upon as being special. It appears that vulgarity in our language makes us stand out from the crowd and, ironically, it also makes us feel a part of the crowd, especially the more that such language permeates our lives.

In my career in education I have heard many times the voice of idealism. Young people want to make a difference in the world. They want to make this a better place, but they often ask, "What can we possibly do?" I believe we all have individual power to make significant differences on this spinning earth. This power rests in the immediate world that surrounds us.

I tell young people that if they want to feed the hungry, they ought to bake their parents a loaf of homemade bread and present it to them on their weary return from a long day's work. If teenagers want to help the poor, they ought to find someone who really can't afford a beautiful dress for the prom and do something about it. If they want to help people who are not as blessed as they are, they ought to volunteer at a local Special Olympics event. If seventeen-year-old students want to clean up the environment, I suggest that they pick up some trash on their way home from school. And if they wish to redecorate the world, they can erase the graffiti from their daily conversations.

Oh, I know that many teenagers who read this will say that these actions are corny, uncool, sentimental, stupid, but I really believe we can make individual, significant contributions on a daily basis. Of course, as they grow older, they will realize that loving their wives and husbands, loving their children, and loving their friends are eventually the best contributions that they can make.

Many young people who read this will sneer, laugh, swear, crumble this up, and move on with their lives, but I think there are some who just might change. We are trying very hard in this society to create a smoke-free environment. Perhaps we can also make an attempt at creating a vulgar-free society.

The English language is just one of the many, extraordinary, beautiful parts of our lives. I think we human beings ought to preserve what is beautiful whenever we can.

Eliot heard the mermaids singing, each to each. I listen to the sound of my mother reading her poetry. I listen to my nine-year-old son Michael reciting the events of his day, and I continue to look forward to hearing young, clear, powerful, bright voices in the hallway outside my office.

Beauty born of beauty breeds beauty in every way.

During the time when John was baptizing those who wished to be baptized, there was a concern among the people that someone else was pretending to be the One who could baptize, and the people were concerned and a bit puzzled.

John reassured the people that *a man can receive only what is given him from heaven* (John 3:27). A person who is given words of beauty is a person who will express beauty. A person who is given words of ugliness will express what is ugly. All beauty can be traced, ultimately, to God.

In our lives we wait with great anticipation for good news. *The friend who attends the bridegroom waits and listens for him, and is full of joy when he hears the bridegroom's voice* (John 3:29).

Suggest today to your children or to those you work with that such grace there is in the voice of those who speak with grace.

I thank You, Lord, for language, for the ability to speak in whispers and in shouts of joy. I thank You for my ability to sing. I sing in the name of the Lord.

The Coming of the Lord

And there were shepherds living out in the fields nearby, keeping watch over their flocks at night. An angel of the Lord appeared to them, and the glory of the Lord shone around them, and they were terrified. But the angel said to them, "Do not be afraid."
LUKE 2:8–10

Suppose an angel of the Lord appeared before us and announced there was great news? "A baby is born, an extraordinary baby who is the Savior. The holy One. The salvation of all people."

I suppose we would want to see such a Child. The shepherds in the field that night over two thousand years ago were probably tired after a long day's tending to their sheep. They were awakened in the middle of the night by an angel, and then a full collection of heavenly hosts appeared in praise of God and the event of wonders.

I sometimes think about the appearance of the angels to these people. This morning after I shut off the alarm clock, I leaned over my bed and looked out my window toward the east. The sky was rose and pink and blue and yellow. The horizon was illuminated. I shook my wife's shoulder and whispered, "Roe, look at the morning."

"I want to sleep a bit more."

"But the light. It is beautiful."

I am no astronomer. There are people who can explain light, sun, distance, energy. I understand warmth on my face. I understand the movement of clouds passing slowly along the soft edge of the morning: giant clouds, thin clouds, ships billowing out beyond the backyard fence.

The shepherds were not afraid of the heavenly guest who descended upon them; they just wanted to go to Bethlehem and see what had happened.

"The sun, Roe. The morning." I nearly wished that she and I could sit on the edge of our bed and fly up with the clouds and be a part of the sunrise.

The shepherds did not realize that they would forever be a part of the sunrise. When they told everyone what they had seen in Bethlehem, their listeners were astonished.

I wish I had been among the shepherds in that field that night. "Yes. We saw an infant wrapped in a blanket. He was peaceful. His mother was grateful that we had come. She sat on the floor of the stable. She looked as if she was in thought. I cannot guess what was in her heart, but I can tell you that the infant moved his hands."

"All of the Eastern seaboard of the United States is waking up, Roe, in a single gesture from the sunlight against the sky." She smiled.

Happy the shepherds in the field on their way home from their journey to Bethlehem. Let us be happy as we wake up this morning to make our way to the entrance of that stable to stand under the Infant's hands moving before us in a blessing.

In the poverty of the stable, the richness was found. In the poverty of my heart, I pray that the Lord Jesus can be found. Holy Child, holy Innocence. Let me carry such a Child and innocence out from Bethlehem each day.

God's Home

"How dare you turn my Father's house into a market!"

John 2:16

The house in Brussels, Belgium, where my father grew up no longer exists. There is, in its place, a city parking lot. No one consulted me when it was decided to knock it down. No one thought it important that the rooms where my grandparents lived would be of interest someday to a grandson in America.

We go through our lives remembering favorite places. We sometimes return to these places only to find out that they no longer exist, that they have been ruined somehow.

Look what we as a nation have done to Henry David Thoreau's famous Walden Pond. We try to preserve it as Thoreau knew it, but highways, stores, and homes surround the area.

What place is sacred? Movie stars press their hand- and footprints into a Hollywood sidewalk. Historical plaques are placed at the site of terrible events: the killing of President Kennedy, for example. We treat our cemeteries, our homes, our yards, our famous city buildings with respect.

We guard a place that has meaning to us. Can you imagine how angry Jesus must have been when He discovered *men selling cattle, sheep and doves, and others sitting at tables exchanging money* in the temple courts (John 2:14)?

I remember that when I was a boy, I once turned my head around to watch the people entering the church. An old woman sitting behind me thumped my head with her knuckles and said, "Show respect in God's house, young man. Turn around."

Well, today I realize that the old woman was out of line a bit in whacking me on the head, but her sentiment was something to admire. She had such reverence for the church, for the house of God, that she felt that children should face the front and not show any hint of disrespect.

Jesus was full of anger when He saw that people weren't treating the temple in the way He felt it ought to be treated. *He made a whip out of cords, and drove all from the temple area, both sheep and cattle; he scattered the coins of the money changers and overturned their tables. To those who sold doves he said, "Get these out of here! How dare you turn my Father's house into a market!"* (John 2:15–16).

Perhaps you can stop by your church sometime this week and regard it with renewed affection. Perhaps you could ask your minister or priest if you could rake the leaves around the church, or wash the church windows, or buy some fresh flowers to be placed by the pulpit.

I bet God loves flowers, neatly raked yards, and clean windows at His house. And while you are busy with these household chores, look over your shoulder now and then and say a prayer as you take a backward glimpse at the church, or the altar, and be careful that someone doesn't whack your head with her knuckles.

In the home of my heart, I find You, Lord. In the home of my church, I praise You. In the home of my family, I hear You, Lord. In the home of my death, I will embrace You.

Do Not Fear the Truth

Whoever lives by the truth comes into the light, so that it may be seen plainly that what he has done has been done through God.
                                                                    JOHN 3:21

I have been accused of being an optimist. Some people have called me naive. Some people believe that I see only what is good in the world and refuse to see what is ugly. I believe it is the man who sees the ugliness but is still able to sing who has the better vision. Forgive my singing.

The very first time I was introduced to something ugly was when I was eleven years old and in the sixth grade. I had transferred to a new school because my parents weren't happy with the school I was attending at the time. This new school was in the next town, a small church school at the top of a hill.

During one of my first days at this school I was standing by myself on the playground when two eighth-grade boys walked up to me and invited me into the woods with them. Hoping for new friends, I joined them.

There was a path leading into the woods. As we began to walk, I began to feel that perhaps my new school would not be so terrible after all. After we walked for a few moments, the boys stopped and pointed at a dress on the ground. They began to giggle. I didn't understand, but I giggled too.

"Pick it up," one boy said.

I picked up the dress. The boys laughed.

"Now roll it up and take it back to school."

I didn't understand. "What should I do with it?"

"Stuff it in your book bag, and don't tell anyone."

I rolled the dress up into a tight ball, tucked it under my arm and followed the boys out of the woods just as a teacher blew a whistle.

I ran back into the school, quickly found my book bag in the back closet, dumped the dress in the front pocket, and walked to my desk. The day continued: math, reading, spelling, and then the principal of the school entered the classroom. He whispered something to the teacher, then he called out my name.

"Yes, sir?" I asked as I stood up from my desk.

"Follow me."

I walked down the aisle. I walked by my classmates, as they watched me with curiosity. When I reached the hallway, the principal motioned with his index finger and said, "Follow me."

To this day I do not know why he led me into the boiler room; at least I think it was a boiler room. I remember brooms, pipes, red machinery. The principal shut the door behind us, then asked in a stern voice, "Where did you see a naked girl?"

I looked up at this man and had no idea what he was talking about.

"Tell me, and you won't be in as much trouble as you will be if you don't tell me."

"I didn't see anyone," I quietly said.

"I know about the woods," he leaned over me.

"The woods?" I asked.

The door to the boiler room opened, and my teacher stepped in with my book bag. She handed the bag to the principal and left. That is when the principal screamed "When did you see the naked girl?

Tell me, you horrible boy!" He shook his fist in my face, and then he reached into my book bag and pulled out the dirty dress.

When I began to cry, he thought, for sure, that I was guilty. Between sobs, I stuttered the names of the two boys I met at recess, explained about the woods and the path and how they told me to take the dress, and why I did. The principal looked at me with disgust and pushed me out into the hall. "Stay here," he ordered.

The big man walked down the hall and entered my classroom. Seconds later, the two boys I had met were walking behind the principal. As they passed me, they sneered with anger and satisfaction. The principal growled at me, "Go back to class."

I walked to the door of the classroom, looked in, and saw that everyone, including the teacher, was waiting for me. I returned to my desk, sat down, and buried my head in my arms.

I never saw those two boys again, and the principal never spoke to me for the rest of the year. The next year I was transferred again to another school.

When Nicodemus, a member of the ruling council, asked Jesus about the notion of being reborn, Jesus said, "*We speak of what we know, and we testify to what we have seen, but still you people do not accept our testimony. I have spoken to you of earthly things and you do not believe; how then will you believe if I speak of heavenly things?*" (John 3:11–12).

How is it that truth can be so elusive? A small boy stood as a victim to the prank of two older boys, and there was never an apology from the principal. I was so frightened in that boiler room. Moreover, I still see his fist in my face.

Jesus was trying to explain to Nicodemus that *men loved darkness instead of light because their deeds were evil. Everyone who does evil hates the light, and will not come into the light for fear that his deeds will be exposed* (John 3:19–20).

Today as you go to work, do not fear the truth. Do not fear the light. Is there something you have done that you are carrying as a burden? Confess to the Lord and ask forgiveness. That is all, and you will be forgiven.

Lift the cross from my shoulder, Lord. Oh, lift the cross. Help me, Lord, for I need Your help and everlasting love.

May God Protect Us and Forgive Us

If any of you is without sin, let him be the first to throw a stone . . .
JOHN 8:7

What small deaths in your own life did you have to endure before you felt that you finally rose up and became a whole person?

All the children in my first grade class were divided into three reading groups: robins, rabbits, and turtles. I suppose the robins soared above everyone else; the rabbits could not quite fly yet, but they were pretty fast; and the turtles, well, no one ever said outright what the turtles could do, but we all knew. I was told that I was a turtle.

In seventh grade I wanted to be on the safety patrol. Children had to be elected to that post by their classmates; then they could wear the yellow belts that slipped around their waists and shoulders.

Brian Olsen was elected year after year to the safety patrol, as were Jack, Cara, Jason, Shawn, Nancy, and Kendra. I was never elected.

In high school there was a party. Tom, my best friend at the time, and I decided to see what was going on. We, in our blue jeans and T-shirts, drove to Kendra's house, rang the doorbell, and waited.

After a correct moment, the door opened, and there stood Kendra in a semiformal dress. I could see deep inside her house. Jack,

Jason, and Shawn wore jackets and ties. Nancy sat on a couch with a tall, thin glass in her hand.

"Ah," Kendra began. "I'm afraid this is a party by invitation only, you guys." What she was really saying is that Tom and I weren't good enough.

When I was a senior in high school, my guidance counselor said that I shouldn't bother to apply to any colleges, because I wouldn't be accepted.

For twelve years in school I was told that I didn't measure up, that I wasn't good enough, that I didn't belong with the regular students, that I didn't hang around with the right kids. For twelve years in school I was identified year after year as a weak speller, a slow reader, a poor math student, and I was tracked into the bottom classes.

Do you know what it does to a child when he hears he is stupid? The "S" word is never stated in schools by teachers or administrators. You will never find the "S" word on any official school records, but children have an amazing sense to understand guilt by association: remedial education, tracking, general math, basic English.

I have been a high school English teacher for the past fifteen years. Yesterday morning I stepped into my classroom to write some vocabulary words on the board before the students arrived. I walked up to the front of the room and was about to place my briefcase down on the side of my chair when I found, stretched out like a happy yellow snake, a safety patrol belt. I had told my students the day before that I once wanted to be a part of something when I was a child, something important in the eyes of others, like the safety patrol. As my students sat down for the vocabulary lesson, I began looking for a certain smile on the face of one of my students, and there he was: Michael.

"I was on the safety patrol many years ago," he confessed, "and I never turned in my belt. You can keep it, Mr. de Vinck."

I have a doctorate from Columbia University and have published books with Doubleday and Viking. My third book will be published by Macmillan in October. I have written articles for the *Wall Street Journal,* the *New York Times,* the *American Scholar,* the *College Board Review,* but none of these accomplishments mean as much to me as the gesture of humor and kindness created by my sixteen-year-old student. I wore that safety patrol belt all day.

It has taken me many, many years to repair the damage that my elementary and high school experience did to my self-esteem.

We do not practice true democratic ideals in many of our school systems across the country. There is a clear aristocracy in the classrooms, perpetuated through the leveling of children.

Tracking students in grammar school and in high school is wrong. Labeling students is wrong.

I am *not* a turtle.

John the Baptist, during the last months before his death, was creating an extraordinary name for himself by following the way of Jesus and baptizing those who came to him. *Some were saying, "John the Baptist has been raised from the dead, and that is why miraculous powers are at work in him."*

Others said, "He is Elijah."

And still others claimed, "He is a prophet, like one of the prophets of long ago" (Mark 6:14–15).

We all, eventually, create a reputation about who we are and about what we are doing on this earth. It is a sad thing when that reputation is hurt along the way by well-intentioned people, like the people in my schools when I was a child. I knew I was a nice person and not dumb, because my mother and father told me so, yet every day I spent in school from first to twelfth grade I felt I wasn't very smart, and if I wasn't very smart, I reasoned, then I probably was not such a nice person.

John the Baptist was a good man, an extraordinary man, yet there were those who wanted to harm him. His goodness stood face-to-face with those who were not so good. He who is evil pleases the Devil, and he who is good is the Devil's enemy.

Innocence is in danger before those who have power. *Herod himself had given orders to have John arrested, and he had him bound and put in prison. He did this because of Herodias, his brother Philip's wife, whom he had married. For John had been saying to Herod, "It is not lawful for you to have your brother's wife." So Herodias nursed a grudge against John and wanted to kill him. But she was not able to, because Herod feared John and protected him, knowing him to be a righteous and holy man. When Herod heard John, he was greatly puzzled; yet he liked to listen to him.*

Finally the opportune time came. On his birthday Herod gave a banquet for his high officials and military commanders and the leading men of Galilee. When the daughter of Herodias came in and danced, she pleased Herod and his dinner guests.

The king said to the girl, "Ask me for anything you want, and I'll give it to you." And he promised her with an oath, "Whatever you ask I will give you, up to half my kingdom."

She went out and said to her mother, "What shall I ask for?"

"The head of John the Baptist," she answered.

At once the girl hurried to the king with the request: "I want you to give me right now the head of John the Baptist on a platter."

The king was greatly distressed, but because of his oaths and his dinner guests, he did not want to refuse her. So he immediately sent an executioner with orders to bring John's head. The man went, beheaded John in the prison, and brought back his head on a platter (Mark 6: 17–28).

When I was a child in school, I felt left out and ignored. There is someone in your life who is hurting deeply inside but is not showing it. You have the ground sense necessary to understand who this person is. Perhaps you can offer this person a kind word of encouragement. Perhaps you can offer this person help. Or perhaps you can pray for this person. Such intervention will make a difference.

Forgive, oh, Lord, those who do harm to others, for they do not know what they are doing. Teach me how to forgive. Lift anger and vengeance from my heart.

Prayer and Song

My house will be called a house of prayer.
MATTHEW 21:13

In ancient times, people prayed to the sun or to the living spirits in trees and flowers. Until science was created, people believed that wolves could turn into men and that the sea gave off an essence that could cure us from death.

Now, it seems, more and more of our physical world is being explained through the use of microscopes, computers, and research. And our prayers? Well, perhaps they, too, have been placed into our modern world into neat packages, copyrighted by the vicar or priest or by a midwestern publishing conference that convenes once every three years to determine the best prayers for local congregations.

Are we teaching our children to pray to the formula: chants, rhymes, church words held together in tradition that become routine and meaningless?

For years I have listened to certain prayers in my church, and I have sung the songs. They do not mean as much to me today after I heard, on two different occasions, a song and a prayer that stand out among all the songs and prayers I have ever heard, and both experiences happened while I visited my writer friend, Father Henri Nouwen.

Many years ago I was working for the Christophers in New York City, an interfaith organization that promotes goodness under their motto: "It is better to light one candle than to curse the darkness." Following the annual Christopher awards ceremony, I was standing in line, waiting to retrieve my coat. Standing before me was a tall, thin man with curled, dark hair. It was Henri. We struck up a conversation.

We became fast friends, Henri and I. He invited me to spend some days with him and his students in Cambridge. For three days Henri cooked my meals, made my bed, invited me to his morning prayers, to his meals, to his classroom. In one class I sat in the back of the room as students began entering the classroom. There seemed to be over a hundred Harvard students taking their seats.

Henri stood before the class, spoke some words of greeting, introduced me to his students—and then something happened. I don't know if Henri gave a signal, or if this was a prearranged routine, but a young man stood up before the class, raised his hand, and the class began to sing.

Harvard University? Singing? I had never before heard the music of Taize, and I was never to hear it again with such beauty as that time I listened to those young people sing. "I taught them to do this," Henri whispered as he sat beside me, singing the loudest.

Henri is my friend perhaps because we are both writers and we do not have to explain too much to each other, for there is a quick and mutual recognition that connects all writers.

As the years moved along, Henri and I kept up a correspondence. We sent each other our newest books and articles published. We endured and shared our successes and struggles.

Then Henri moved to a place called Daybreak, a community of people joined together by mutual needs. Some people there need to be fed by hand. Some people cannot speak or think. Some of the adults have the intellect of five-year-old children. But all the people of Daybreak are blessed to have found their way into a community that is founded upon the acceptance of the power of the Holy Spirit. Daybreak is a place where faith in God and in God's love sustains the people who cook, who change diapers, who carry mentally disabled people from their beds to tubs of warm water for a daily bath.

Fred Rogers and I visited Daybreak together to spend some time with Henri. On the evening of our first day, Henri invited us to the daily Mass held in the late afternoon. Fred and I sat at Henri's right as he began, "My brothers and sisters, we are gathered here this afternoon to celebrate the Eucharist together."

There were old people in wheelchairs, young people in braces. Some of the people in the little chapel were drooling; some were rocking their heads back and forth. I saw people holding the songbooks in their hands and reading; some were sitting on the floor with their eyes closed—people with big heads, people with no intellect, people with Down's syndrome, people with severe brain damage.

At one point, Henri spoke about prayer, then he asked everyone in the congregation to offer individual, personal prayers of petition. A young woman with Down's syndrome prayed for her friend who was not feeling well that day. The man with a large head offered a prayer for Fred Rogers and that he might make many more children's television visits in the Neighborhood.

Then a young man who was sitting cross-legged on the floor began his prayer. He could not have been over twenty years old, and it was obvious that he had been born with severe brain damage. This young man sat in the middle of the floor, with everyone watching and listening. He began his prayer. He could not speak, but he could make guttural noises with his mouth and vocal cords. This man began to pray with conviction in a chant-like fashion. No one could understand what he was saying. And on and on his odd-sounding prayer continued.

The sound of this young man's "voice" startled me, for he was praying the most beautiful prayer I had ever heard. There were no words, but there was God and faith and courage and goodness and sorrow in this man's voice.

When I first met Henri, I didn't know who he was. I thought he was a nice fellow receiving a new award for some nice things he had done with his life. I didn't know that Henri was the new Thomas Merton. I didn't know that Henri's books on spirituality were read by millions of people. I didn't know that Henri was invited all over the world to speak. I didn't know that Henri was to be one of the holiest men I would ever meet.

I also didn't know that Henri would introduce me to the most beautiful songs I have ever heard and to the most profound prayers I am likely to ever hear.

What is your favorite song and prayer? Do you sing and pray in the morning? Fall into the habit of singing and praying, and you will fall into a new dialogue with the Lord.

We belong to God; we belong in His house. In His house there is prayer and song. To You, my God, I sing and pray. I accept Your invitation. I am coming closer each day with my song and prayer. The doors, the doors, open the doors.

God of Light

You are my lamp, O LORD; the LORD turns my darkness into light.

2 SAMUEL 22:29

At what exact point does the day give up its hold on the light and wave surrender to the oncoming night? At a certain point I find myself turning on the lamps in the living room, yet the backyard is not engulfed in full darkness.

When I was a child and the days were seamless, I kept a close watch on the light in the garden. It was the garden of my childhood, a place for apple blossoms and daylilies, irises and roses, and exotic ferns the size of elephant ears.

During the summers when my grandparents came to visit from Belgium, the garden belonged to my grandfather, the man who had been a general in the army and the same man who, in retirement, planted his knees into the soil as he bent over and planted pansies.

The morning light skimmed over the maple trees from the east, melting the darkness from the tips of each tree. Light dripped into the ferns and splashed onto the grass, spreading up to the house. I liked to dip my bare feet into the sunlight as it made its way onto the back porch.

The afternoon light suggested an illuminated theater, all the scenery ablaze in preparation for the matinee performance. The stone wall, the trellis, the ferns were equally lit, center stage. I was a bit player, walking among the stars.

It was, however, the early evening light that caused me the most delight. I liked how the sun's amber cast itself inside the house, particularly through the upstairs window. This light was an end-of-day light, the beginning of a farewell.

I had a dream last night about my grandfather. He was standing beside a fence. On the other side of the fence was a white horse. I assumed that the horse belonged to my grandfather. He was standing in his uniform. His boots were dirty. He waved me over toward him.

I was always a bit afraid of my grandfather. He was appalled that I bit my fingernails and often angered that I didn't respond quickly enough to his orders, but he was a good man, a man of integrity and intellect who loved his grandchildren. He would kiss my sisters and brothers and me good-night. "Good-night, boy," he would say. I wish my grandfather had lived to see me as a man.

In my dream my grandfather saluted as I approached him, so I saluted back. "Stand still," he ordered. I did as I was told in my dreams. My grandfather leaned over, grabbed my waist with his two hands, and lifted me above his head. I must have been six or seven in this dream. I do not remember being lifted as a child. We are too small to keep such a clear memory, but the feeling of being held by those we love is a feeling we must retain the rest of our lives, for it seems to be something we seek again and again.

In my dream my grandfather passed me over the fence and placed me on the back of the white horse.

"Hold on to the hair on the back of its neck."

The horse didn't have a saddle. I remember the fear. I remember feeling high off the ground. My grandfather clapped his hands and the horse stepped backward, then began to walk in a circle.

The sun was situated behind my grandfather, so my dream must have taken place at the end of the day. I could not imagine riding a horse at dawn. Each time I rode around and around, my grandfather would appear and disappear in the glare of the sun's light. I would turn to him and squint my eyes, trying to see him as the horse carried me in faster and faster circles.

Dreams we create at night seem to suggest mixed messages, hidden meanings, possible suggestions of our inner thoughts that bubble up only in the dark when we are sleeping, when we can imagine things that are unimaginable in the light of day. My grandfather paid more attention to the zinnias and marigolds than he did to me. But in my dream he placed me on a white horse, a cavalry horse, the general's horse. I, the general's son.

My dream ended as most dreams end, in the morning light, in the call of the new day's responsibilities: a daughter and two sons to wake, a wife to kiss in greeting, the dog to walk, the workday to conquer. We are creatures of the sun, trained to heed its cycle. The light reveals a new truth each day.

I am a watcher of the light. I have been trained in the yard of my childhood. I accept the passing time, lost shadows, the fading of the light. I grow old. There are no more flowers in the garden. Even though the sun becomes each year more and more just a yellow light, just an ordinary occurrence, I still try to keep the warmth against my cheeks carried over from those long-ago days. And last night, I liked the ride upon that horse in the light of my grandfather's approving wave.

This evening take notice of the waning sun's light against the tips of trees. Listen to the songbirds' lament, dream of youth, accept the passing of time, and give thanks to the Lord for another day in His radiance.

No sun, no crown of gold is more radiant than God's love. Love me, God. Press Your light against my open face. I am warm in Your presence. Protect me when I am cold. Protect me when I am in darkness, God of light, God of gold, God of love, have mercy on me.

God the Father, Our Protector

He protected us on our entire journey.

When I return to my bed for the evening, when the children are asleep and my wife is sleeping, I lie down and pull the covers up to my neck. Could they be a shroud? A veil to hide myself behind? A flag of defeat draped against my body in surrender to the day's battle?

Children feel more protected under the covers. Before Roe and I married, I slept under a heavy quilted blanket and a cat. Roe doesn't like heavy quilted blankets or cats on the bed. I'd rather sleep with Roe than with a heavy quilted blanket and a cat, so the blanket was sold in a garage sale and the cat sleeps in the children's room.

I have always felt the need for protection, from the time I was pushed against the outside wall of the school building when I was eight to the times I was taunted by a mean-spirited soccer player in high school, the boy who was so quick with his feet and his tongue, lashing out at those who could not run or play soccer or challenge him with like bravado.

I have lived a life under the protection of my mother and father, then under the protection of Roe and our children. How little the children understand that they protect their father. They keep me from driving west and never stopping. They help me keep the bread drawer full. My daughter tells me that she loves me. My boys want to play

Monopoly. We drape ourselves with shields. Roe keeps the thieves of loneliness away from me, except when I am alone in the car, when I drive to work, or when I return. There is no one in the car, so I imagine former bullies, former images of people I loved and thought I loved, who all seem to haunt the empty seat beside me as I stop at traffic lights, adjust the radio, push my foot on the accelerator.

In my bed in the deep, late hours of the night, I feel the light blanket against my legs. I listen for the distant freight train that does not come. I hear Roe breathing. There is an occasional car that illuminates the far wall for a moment, a yellow screen of light, projecting images of a little boy cutting his knee open in a fall from his bicycle, and there is a man, a tall man carrying the boy to the house. The man is my father, though he does not say a word. Boys need the protection of their fathers. Without the father, the son cannot be brave all his life.

Last spring, Roe and I were riding our bicycles. We wheeled down the driveway, turned left, and headed for the golf course. I do not play golf, but I enjoy visiting the local fields that are green and smooth and clean and bright and placed at the foot of low hills.

We rode and we rode, side by side or in single file, depending on the width of the road and the traffic. When we reached the small street leading up to the fairways, Roe suggested that we, after all, not continue. "The road is too steep."

I suggested that we walk the bicycles up to the golf course. "I'd like to see the grass and how it leads up into the hills. I like how that looks."

Roe agreed to follow, and we slowly leaned into our task. After fifteen minutes we were at the top of the hill looking down at the county park. Some people were on the green. Some were standing beside the clubhouse, waiting. I watched as a crow circled the sixth hole once and disappeared around a distant tree. "Okay. I've seen it. Let's go home."

Roe and I turned our bicycles toward the steep incline we had just conquered. "Let's walk down," Roe wisely suggested.

"Not me! Not after I worked so hard getting here in the first place. I'll meet you at the bottom," I said as I mounted the bicycle, placed my feet on the two pedals, and shot down the hill.

Roe called out, "Slow down! Remember, the main street is at the bottom!"

I turned to look at her with my sense of courage and disdain. Of course, I knew what I was doing. *What is the matter with her?* But then I saw car after car rolling past the entrance at the bottom of the hill and realized that I was traveling much too fast and would have to slow down so as not to zoom into the speeding cars.

I exerted pressure on the foot brakes when suddenly the bicycle chain broke, and I was without any mechanical way to stop. The bicycle and I were out of control. I surely didn't want to crash into a car traveling at forty miles an hour, so I quickly turned the bicycle into the grass that led up toward the woods. The bicycle shook as it rolled onto the grass. There was less speed, but I was now heading toward the trees, so I simply tipped over and fell onto the grass with the bicycle on my back.

Roe said later that she didn't know whether to laugh or cry, for the scene before her looked funny: her silly husband rushing down the hill and flipping over into the grass like a crazed stunt actor, clown, foolish man who had been warned not to sail down the hill with no concern.

My side was scraped. My leg was bleeding. I broke my right hand. Not since I was a teenager had I broken a bone.

After the doctor snapped X rays, diagnosed the break, and wrapped my hand, I stepped from his office—and I was afraid. I looked at the bandage and the splint. I tried to wiggle my fingers, but they hurt too much.

How small are the hints of our own mortality? My hand healed within six weeks. My bicycle is twisted and bent beyond repair. I am now, for the first time in my life, afraid of being injured.

At night when I am restless, I wrap the blanket tightly around my body.

It is okay to be afraid. We human beings were taught to be cautious, to avoid injury, to protect ourselves. What you fear today might very well be the thing you should fear and avoid. But remember, as you stand up against what you are afraid of, Jesus is standing right beside you. He is there always to protect you and guide you. Trust in the Lord, for He is good.

When I am weak, Your strength carries me across the day. When I am lonely, Your company helps pass the time. When I am hungry, You divide the loaves. Dear Lord, Father-protector, thank You for remembering me. Thank You for keeping me safe.

A Mother's Extraordinary Gifts

As a mother comforts her child, so will I comfort you.

ISAIAH 66:13A

"You must prepare yourself for the adult world," a teacher announced to my high school class when I was fifteen. She was our new health teacher, hoping to convince us that if we learn about polite, clean, educated, hard-working people in the community we would also someday become a part of the adult world. I thought there was more to being an adult than cleanliness and education.

I wanted to buy a school football jacket because it seemed obvious that the most popular boys in the school wore these wonderful, heavy, black jackets with white imitation-leather sleeves.

At the end of the day I walked to the school store. I waited until the afternoon rush of candy buyers paid for their end-of-the-day snacks, then I stepped into the room and walked up to the counter, where a gym teacher stood. He leaned over and asked, "Can I help you?"

Behind the man a tall, glass case displayed the various school jackets for sale.

"I'd like to buy a school coat." I didn't even have the money. I hadn't thought that far ahead. I just knew that once I wore the jacket, everything would take care of itself: money problems, my loneliness, my isolation from the other students.

I can explain why I was so left out of things during my first years of high school. I was not good at any sports. I was reserved. I was a poor student. No one seemed to care.

"What coat would you like?" the teacher asked me.

I inspected the coats in the display case, then with certitude I pointed to the black coat with the white sleeves.

The man lifted his pencil and began asking me questions as he began to fill out an order form. "Name."

"Christopher de Vinck."

"How do you spell that?"

"C-h-r-i-s-t-o . . ."

"Ah," the man mumbled. "How do you spell your last name?"

"D-e-V-i-n-c-k."

"Is that a B?" he asked?

"My name is de Vinck. Christopher. Christopher de Vinck."

"How do you spell your last name? Is it de Binck or de Vinck?"

How, I asked myself, *could this man not know the difference?* "Vinck. V. Like victory. I've been going to this school for almost a year."

"Glad to meet you." The man licked the tip of his pencil. "What size do you want?"

I hadn't thought about that. I had never bought a coat before because I was always given my older brother's coat when he outgrew the neighbor's hand-me-down. "What sizes do you have?"

The man looked at me and slapped his pencil down. "Small," he breathed loudly, "medium, or large."

I wanted to say *large*, for boys of fifteen like to be big and strong, but I settled for "Medium. I wear a medium."

59

The teacher lifted his pencil and continued to write on the order form. "All right. Now which coat do you want?"

"That one," I pointed. "The black one. The one with the white sleeves." I wanted to add—"The one all the other guys are wearing"—but I didn't.

"Okay," the teacher continued. "What was your varsity sport?"

"What?" I asked.

"Your sport. What varsity sport did you play? What's your number?"

I didn't know what the man was talking about. At that time I didn't know what "varsity" meant, and I didn't know why he asked about a number.

"My phone number?" *Did he want to know my phone number?*

"Son, what sport did you play?"

"I never played any sports," I answered naively.

"The coat you want is for the boys who play a sport and earn a varsity position on a team."

"What's 'varsity' mean?"

The teacher looked down at me and placed his pencil on the counter for the last time.

"Obviously you haven't earned a varsity letter, young man. But if you like, you can order this coat," and he pointed to a black-and-red coat without the white sleeves, the coat that none of the popular boys wore. "It is even less expensive than the one you wanted."

As I walked home, I couldn't understand why it was that some people seemed to have so many friends while others—well, they just did the best they could. It started to rain. I pulled my jacket over my head. By the time I reached my home, I was drenched.

I walked in the front door. My mother was in the kitchen. She called me. "Chrissy, come have some spice cake. It is so good to see you." When I walked into the kitchen, my mother kissed me. "How was your day?"

I wanted to tell her about the coat, but somehow the cake made it seem not so important after all.

Mothers sometimes never know what extraordinary gifts they are to their children just at the right moment. Do you remember a time that your mother did something for you, or said something to you that made all the difference? Write your mother a letter, or call her on the phone. Remind her of that moment long ago when she lifted your spirits. She will be grateful that you told her so.

Lord of the family, we thank You for the encouragement You give us each day. Lord of wisdom and grace, we thank You for the mothers of the world who know how to encourage us in the name of hope and strength.

May our Lord Jesus Christ himself and God our Father, who loved us and by his grace gave us eternal encouragement and good hope, encourage your hearts and strengthen you in every good deed and word (2 Thessalonians 2:16–17).

What Is Real and What Is False

Do nothing out of selfish ambition or vain conceit.
PHILIPPIANS 2:3

I read an announcement in the *New York Times* concerning another autograph show to be conducted at one of New York City's most elegant hotels. For years I was hoping to find an autograph of my favorite author, the New Jersey poet William Carlos Williams.

During my many years in college and during my many years as a high school English teacher, I was expected to read classical literature, American and British literature, literature of various cultures and languages. I read poems, plays, novels, short stories, essays. Some books informed me, some entertained. Some books angered me, some brought me much peace and stability. But no book, no single author consistently brought me to a place of sudden revelations and intimate connections to what I hope to accomplish in my own life than the poetry of Williams.

William Carlos Williams was a family doctor who spent his entire life in Rutherford, New Jersey, tending to sick children, visiting old men and women, delivering babies, waking up in the night to a phone call from a patient in need. Williams lived a part of his life in the practical, broken world that he tried, in his own way, to repair with his healing hands and with his medical degree. He also stole minutes and hours amid the stress of his life to create poems that will endure. He liked to visit New York City, spending time with writers and painters, keeping, for a moment, a distance from his family and from his patients.

He was a man divided: a man who lived in the world of the common day and a man who lived in the world of his sensitivity, which he developed through his constant attempts to speak through his poetry. We all live many different lives: the lives that people see and the lives that only we feel and endure. We are lucky if we can explain to someone else even a small fraction of what goes on deep inside our significant selves that too often is ignored or, eventually, buried.

William Carlos Williams was able to do with words what painters do with color and images. Williams was able to create a notion and compare that notion with something else. A number of young schoolgirls walking up the street are simply schoolgirls walking up the street until Williams wiggles his pen, adds a few words, and suddenly these girls represent all lost girls who once knew the way to their homes and spring but who have stepped into their womanhood and, well, have left schoolgirl concerns behind, yet there is forever the lasting image of the girls walking together, going somewhere.

Williams taught me that poetry, after all, ought not be held hostage by a few academic critics who hold that the only great poetry is the poetry of a sick and bored nineteenth-century Europe, where verse was created out of an upper-class belief that poetry is the language of the elite, the scholar, the snob.

Williams taught me that Walt Whitman is the common man's hero when it comes to the liberation of poetic form and joy in American literature. Williams taught me that, even today, most people in control of what is published in American poetry think that they are at war with the human heart and that that heart is to be protected and isolated with poetry that is obscure, that does not contain any music, that is written in a narrative form, and that is steeped in darkness and pain. Williams' poetry is clear, musical, simple, of the people, written in the common language.

When I read in the newspaper that once again there was to be an autograph show, I decided, finally, that I would drive into the city and buy a signature of William Carlos Williams.

I explained to Roe what I intended to do. She thought this was a silly idea, but Roe is not the type of wife who prevents her husband from pursuing silly ideas, no matter how right she is (which is most of the time, well, which is all of the time, but what husband wants to admit that?).

As I drove to the city, I thought about the type of signature I wanted: clear, steady, at the bottom of a significant letter if possible, but a simple autograph would do.

The traffic in New York that Sunday afternoon was, as usual, congested. I was lucky, however, and found a parking spot on the street. By the time I arrived at the show, it was already halfway over.

I paid my five dollars and stepped into the large hotel convention room. There were more than a hundred different tables with vendors of any type of autograph you could imagine: movie stars, sports figures, politicians, musicians, artists . . . writers. I walked to the first table that advertised author signatures.

"Do you have any signatures of William Carlos Williams?"

The man behind the table nodded. "I have five or six." He leaned over and pulled out a black folder. As he flipped through the pages, I could see Faulkner, Fitzgerald, Hemingway, Steinbeck, Frost, Sexton. Then he stopped as he turned the folder around toward me. On one page was a photograph of Williams. On the opposite page were four letters and a single signature. The letters cost three and four hundred dollars. The signature was priced at one hundred twenty-five dollars.

I looked. I rubbed my finger over the plastic pages, thinking that William Carlos Williams had spent a few seconds writing his name on this very piece of paper. For so many years I had hoped to someday have such a signature, and I was about to buy it, but then I turned the folder back to the seller, thanked him politely, turned around, walked out of the hotel, stepped back into my car, and drove home.

I realized that there was no possible way I could spend so much money on something that was, after all, not the man.

Williams' poetry caused a profound change in my life. His writing gave me the courage necessary to continue as a writer. His way of looking at the world helped me realize that the way I look at the world is not a fool's vision. I wanted a part of him, his signature, hanging on my wall in a frame, but now I realize that a part of him is inside my own voice, inside the child I once was, inside the husband, father, writer I am. He has given me the signature of his passion, vision, anger, joy, simplicity, courage. These are the signatures I have been collecting all along the way from a man who died when I was thirteen years old, a man who wrote against the grain, who believed in every person, a man who saw the pain in the peace, in the beauty, in the ugly, in the hope, in the tragic.

When I returned home from the city that evening, Roe asked me if I had found what I was looking for. "I sure did," I said, then Roe, the children, and I sat down for dinner.

What are your desires? What do you seek? As you go through your day, examine what you hope for and see if you can discover the truth in what you wish to find. We sometimes find ourselves in the dream. We sometimes destroy ourselves in the accumulation of things that rust, wither, dry up, and eventually disappear.

Love stays. Compassion stays. Mercy stays. God stays. All human objects disintegrate. Today let me be a collector of Your trophies, Lord.

What the Children Tell Us

Continue your love to those who know you.

PSALM 36:10

Many years ago when I was on vacation in Ontario, Canada, with my family, a small incident reminded me that there are moments when we are suddenly struck with wonderment.

I was on a small beach with my children. They were building sand castles. I was reading the poems of William Carlos Williams. Roe was sunbathing.

As the late morning spilled into the early afternoon, we heard a car pull into the driveway of the cabin beyond the trees. A local farmer had arrived to cut down a tree that had been obstructing the view of the river from the cabin's picture window. He lumbered down to the river's edge with his chain saw at his side.

"I've come to cut the tree."

"Yes. We've been waiting. It's the white one, the birch beside the house."

The man tipped his hat, turned, and walked back. The children stopped their play and ran in the man's footsteps.

"I want to see the saw!" David called out.

"I want to see the tree fall!" Michael said.

"I'm going with them," Karen pointed as she ran past my chair.

Roe and I decided to continue our peaceful rest on the river's edge, peaceful until the man pulled the rope to his power saw. *Varrrroom! Varrrroom!*

A few moments later there was a tremendous crash. The tree collapsed like a dying giraffe. One by one the children returned to the beach. They had a sad look in their eyes. I closed my book of poems and asked, "What's wrong?"

"The tree," David said. "It's dead."

"Did the tree feel any pain?" Michael wanted to know.

Karen didn't say anything. She just stooped down beside her sand castle and built another turret.

It is a good thing to recognize for the first time admirable qualities in those we love. When Mary and Joseph presented Jesus to the temple according to the law, Simeon stepped up to the parents and said, "*This child is destined to cause the falling and rising of many in Israel, and to be a sign that will be spoken against, so that the thoughts of many hearts will be revealed. And a sword will pierce your own soul too*" (Luke 2:34–35).

It is easy to imagine how startled Mary and Joseph were by these words from a man who was told by the Holy Spirit that he would not die until he had met the Lord.

Jesus' parents recognized that their Son had extraordinary qualities. How good it was for me to see that my own children felt remorse at the destruction of something beautiful. How extraordinary it must have been for Mary and Joseph to hear from Simeon that their Son was a revealing light.

It is an act of faith to love and serve the Lord. The sand castles. The sand castles. Karen continued to build the sand castles as the farmer cut the white birch into four-foot chunks of firewood.

Take notice of your children today and praise them for their individual strengths and talents.

Lord God, we are Your children. We play in the field of the Lord. We dance in the songs of our lives. How filled with joy, my Lord, we are when we take You up on Your invitation to come join You each day.

The Fear of Death

Fear the LORD and the king, my son, and do not join with the rebellious, for those two will send sudden destruction.
PROVERBS 24:21–22

It is difficult for me to understand what it must be like to live under siege, to fear bombs dropping around my family, to fear the sniper's bullets, to fear the open streets.

A few years ago my wife and I brought the children to a New York state park. It was the fall, when the leaves blushed and the earth was moist with recent rain. We parked the car and quickly found a path leading up the side of a small incline. The children ran ahead of us as I held my wife's hand. The sound of children laughing as they run ahead of me is, I think, one of life's great pleasures.

As the hill began to shoot upward into a more severe incline, the children started to slow down. David, our oldest, looked for fossils. Karen sang the end of a song, and Michael, the youngest, seven at the time, searched for a walking stick.

Just as Roe and I reached the children, there was a tremendous *bang!* throughout the mountainside. A shotgun blast! We did not realize that it was the hunting season. Somewhere off to our right, beyond the few bushes that separated us, another terrific blast from the gun shot out. We all let up a loud cry. "Hey! We're here! Be careful." Then I turned to find my youngest son running back down the path in a crouched position with his hands over his ears. He called out in a pleading voice, "Don't shoot! Please, don't shoot."

I had to run to catch up to him. I embraced Michael and reassured him that the hunter knew we were here and that he wasn't shooting at us. But the child was frightened.

We returned to the parking lot, my family and I, and we drove to the nearest town and bought ice-cream cones.

I cannot imagine what it must have been like for my mother when she was a teenager in Brussels during World War II. I remember my father's telling us children what it was like to hear V–2 rockets (flying bombs) zooming overhead.

Many years ago, when King Herod heard that there was a child born who was a newborn king, he was suspicious and fearful. He intended to kill the child. An angel spoke to Joseph in his dreams and warned him of the danger. Joseph, being a good father, guided his wife and child to Egypt, where his family was safe.

Protect your family. Do what you must. Reach out. You have the power to surround your family with arms of love and safety.

Blessed are the fathers and mothers who protect their children. Blessed are the angels who warn us of evil. Blessed are the weak, for they are to be protected. Blessed are the peacemakers, for they will inherit kind judgment from their ancestors.

Holy Sounds of Grief

I tell you the truth, you will weep and mourn while the world rejoices. You will grieve, but your grief will turn to joy.

JOHN 16:20

What we do not see, we do not understand. When something cries out, we try to identify the need. The unseen cry is a mystery.

When I heard that a neighbor's child was struck by a car as he rode his bicycle, I gasped and felt great concern and worry. The boy sustained minor bruises. He returned to school in two days.

When children are massacred in a distant land and I see their torn bodies on the front page of the newspaper, I look in horror, shake my head, and turn the page. Do we feel compassion only for those who are physically close to us? Why are we not weeping daily for the death of the innocent? Why are we not on our knees, begging God to spare us all from torture, violence, war, and death?

The mercy of God is shrouded in mystery. What does He see that we do not see? What does He understand that holds our ignorance?

I often think about our individual existence, how is it that we have all survived our own birth and childhood. How is it that we are born of our mother and grandmothers. How many human beings had to exist in order for us to be sitting in a chair in the evening, reading the newspaper?

Each day is a victory—each moment of breath a note of celebration to be sung, but we do not sing. We take all for granted. Humble the dead children in their tombs. Silence their shoes at the doorsteps. A kingdom greater than the fields of spring, a holy place holier than a little girl's bedroom where the dolls lean against each other in the darkness, this heaven, this paradise, this salvation we are promised, we are drawn to. We enter into the kingdom of God from His guidance, with His hand in our palm.

How can we understand such a hand? How can we understand the path some of us take? I do not understand the death of the innocent. It is not for me to know the dialogue that passes between them and the Lord. Lord of mercy. Lord of the sun. Sun Lord.

When King Herod (a human king) learned that the wise men had tricked him and journeyed home by way of another route, the king was furious. Still afraid that this newborn king might be dangerous, Herod ordered all the male babies under the age of two years to be killed.

Can you hear the cries of the children? Can you hear the cries of the mothers and fathers? They are all dead now—the mothers of Bethlehem who wept for the massacre of their innocents, the fathers who tried to console the sobbing women—but they could not be consoled.

What is the nature of our grief? What is the nature of our unconsoled hearts? The weeping echoes through the hills. The echoes pierce our hearts over the centuries and find their way into our literature, into the ringing of the bells on Sunday. The sounds of the mothers weeping are the sounds of human suffering, the sound of grief, the sound of puzzlement, the sound of anger. But we shall be consoled in the living God, in the holy place where all sorrow is joy, where all weeping is turned to laughter.

On this earth we claim hints of joy, quick visions of a sunset that are significantly different from other moments of the setting sun.

See if you can make a connection today to your own private grief and to an image that seems to offer you consolation, like the sunlight against the kitchen floor, perhaps. It is the image from the Lord that will guide you.

Lord, accept our pain. Accept our weeping. Help us in our igno-rance. Help us understand the sounds of our own grief.

The Ugly Sneer of Evil

Do not fret because of evil men or be envious of those who do wrong; for like the grass they will soon wither, like green plants they will soon die away.

PSALM 37:1–2

If we believe our enemy is dead, we have lost the war. Evil is always alive and waiting for the weak, the lost, or the faithless.

When I was in third grade, there was a boy in the fifth grade who frightened me. His hair was cut close to his scalp. His face had a sneer, and he pushed me on the playground every morning for many weeks. Once he pushed me so hard into the side of the school that I sprained my right arm to such a degree that it still hurts me thirty-five years later.

As I rested in the doctor's office afterward, I clearly remember saying to myself, *When I get into high school, people will be much nicer.*

In high school there was this boy, Brian, who seemed to live to make my life miserable. He pushed, taunted, sneered. He was not the same boy who had hurt me in the playground of the elementary school, but he was the same type of child.

Well, I said to myself one afternoon when I was walking home, *when I go to college, there surely won't be anyone like Brian.*

In college on my floor in the dorm, I met people who cheated, slept with any willing girl, mugged a priest, ingested drugs. Different people, same sneer.

Of course, I have come across the sneer of evil in graduate school, in my profession of education, in my writing career. To be sure, I've met thousands of people in my lifetime, and most had faces of goodness reflected in their smiles, but a few wore that same, evil sneer.

I often tell my own children that there will always be someone who will try to make beautiful things ugly, but most people are good. We need to stand guard against the nearly invisible ugliness that is always waiting for its chance to push us against the school wall and cause us harm. Joseph seemed to be well-prepared to fight this evil. He seemed to have had an intuition for what was best for his family.

When Herod died and an angel explained to Joseph that it was safe to return to Israel, he packed up his little family and began heading home. Then Joseph heard that Herod's son had become King of Judea. Joseph must have known that the son was like the father: the new generation of that evil sneer, perhaps. Evil is never dead. It just reappears with a different mask.

Joseph brought his family back to Nazareth, hoping, perhaps, that there he might escape for a while from the darkness that threatened his wife and Child.

As you move about today, sway among the wheat of goodness that is kept warm under the sun and moistened with rain.

The drought will surely come, making its attempt at drying the soil, trying to squeeze into the roots of our being, but we people of faith stand in the field of the Lord and anticipate the coming rain that will refresh us.

I bathe in the water of goodness. I drink the water of goodness. I stand in the rain of goodness. Lord, help me today to once again find the moisture of heaven, the drink of salvation, the pool of Your love.

The Will of God

To do your will, O my God, is my desire.

PSALM 40:8

I received a phone call after one of my essays appeared in the *Wall Street Journal.* It was a small essay about the time my daughter, Karen, had undergone surgery for a tumor in her foot to determine whether or not she had cancer. We were grateful that she was free of the disease.

I had mentioned in the article that a kind, Dutch nurse tended to my daughter in the recovery room. A few days later, the phone rang.

The secretary of a man who owned an oil company said that her boss wanted to send my family a wheel of cheese.

"Excuse me?" I asked, a bit puzzled.

"He is an old man, now, living in Florida, but he still keeps the company going. He read your article about your daughter."

I didn't see what any of this had to do with cheese.

"My boss, he is Dutch. You mentioned that the kind nurse was Dutch. He liked that you mentioned the nurse and her gentle ways. I was given instructions that I was to arrange sending you a wheel of cheese. A gift of cheese in Holland is a token of luck. The man I work for, the head of this oil company, wants you to have this cheese."

Three weeks later, a wheel of white cheese was delivered to our house.

Spontaneous acts of goodness have their origin. By mentioning the Dutch accent in my essay, a man who loved his country of origin was compelled to send my family a wheel of cheese that took us a month to finish. The secretary must have thought that the gesture was a bit odd.

I read in the newspaper where an industrialist was giving a speech at a grammar school graduation ceremony in New York City. As this man was reading his speech, he looked up from his text and saw children doomed to be destroyed by street violence, drugs, and poverty. When he finished his speech, he brushed the paper aside and announced to the one hundred eighth-grade students that if they graduated from high school with good grades, he would pay for their college education. The crowd gasped. The children didn't understand at first the meaning of this gesture. Then they applauded.

Why do people do the things that they do? Why do we carry out sudden acts of kindness? Some people might say, well, every now and then we are hit with guilt, or whims, or deeply felt convictions that need to be acted upon. But I think such deeds are born of a different substance.

Do you remember the story in the Bible when Jesus traveled with His parents to Jerusalem, as was the yearly custom? Remember how, once their business was complete, Mary and Joseph began their trip home? When they looked for their Son, He was nowhere to be found. They searched for Him. They waited for Him to catch up. Realizing that He was not coming, they returned to Jerusalem and found their Son preaching in the temple. Remember how angry Joseph and Mary were? Like any good parents, they were at once annoyed that Jesus had run off from them and equally glad that He was found and unhurt.

Mary asked why He had treated her and Joseph this way. And what was Jesus' reply? "*Why were you searching for me? Didn't you know I had to be in my Father's house?*" (Luke 2:49).

"I am going to send that young man a wheel of cheese."

"I am going to pay for your college education."

"I had to be in my Father's house."

I believe that all acts of kindness, all acts of inner obligations stem from God. He has not abandoned us. We have free will, and in that will we choose to pursue notions that enter into our hearts and minds. We choose to pursue goodness or evil. We choose to do nothing in the face of the choices. We all make choices. Jesus felt compelled, at twelve years of age, to follow God's will.

Discover today how good it is to eat the gift of cheese, to watch young people graduate from school with hope. Feel how good it is to preach the word of God in His houses. This morning discover how good it is to read the Bible, and see how much it speaks to your heart.

Rivers know where they are to go. The sun and moon follow their given paths. Lord, I choose to do Your will. I choose to follow where You have been. Stretch out Your hand today so that I may not fall. Stretch out Your hand, oh, my Lord.

Rise Up and Spread the Good News

Come, follow me, and I will make you fishers of men.
MATTHEW 4:19

We are called to the vocation of the Lord in diverse ways. I know a man who was on a fishing trip deep in the woods of Ontario, Canada. He came upon a community of people who devoted their lives to the poor.

This man looked around, listened to the Gospel, heard the people speak about the poor, and he never left. How did this man come into the Lord's work?—"I went fishing."

Jesus is a fisher of men and women. He asks us all the time to come and join Him. I remember when I introduced my wife to my family for the first time. Later that day my grandmother leaned next to me and whispered, "Is she a Christian?" She was, I nodded, and my grandmother smiled. But we are born into different traditions. We are brought to the Lord by different ways, different religions, different songs and powers.

A man of no faith is an unhappy man. We are, in our lifetime, profoundly influenced by events or notions that have dramatic consequences upon our spiritual lives. For me, it was the time I heard the voice of my grandmother for the last time.

Each summer she would come to us from Belgium. July and August were filled with French laughter, for she could speak only

French. We played cards in the evening, sat outside during the day, and read together on the lawn chairs.

I remember one evening when we were playing a French card game. For some reason, I started humming "Stars and Stripes Forever," then my eighty-six-year-old Belgian grandmother started humming it too.

I picked a card from the deck and started humming even louder. Well, she picked a card and started humming even louder. I started tapping on the table and singing. She stood up and continued the melody. Louder and louder we sang until one might have thought that George Washington had stepped out from the kitchen to congratulate us on our patriotism.

At the end of the song, my grandmother and I sat down, and she asked, "Is it your turn, or mine?"

We both laughed and laughed.

In midwinter of the year my grandmother was ninety-two, we received a phone call from Belgium telling us that my grandmother was in the hospital and near death.

Taking a chance, I called long-distance information, gave the name of the hospital in Brussels, dialed the number, and asked to speak to my grandmother. By a stroke of luck, she was able to speak on the phone. I could barely hear her, but I was able to say, "It's me! Christopher! From America."

All she was able to say was, "Ah, Christopher. I love you," then a nurse interrupted to say that that was all my grandmother was able to say. I thanked the nurse and hung up the phone. My grandmother died the next day and was buried beside my grandfather, a general in the Belgian army who had died ten years before she did.

I heard the words. I heard her say she loved me—her last words to me. My grandmother loved me. It is easy to rise to love when we are loved.

When the word of God came to John the Baptist, *he went into all the country around the Jordan, preaching a baptism of repentance for the forgiveness of sins* (Luke 3:3).

People suspected that this man might be the Christ they had heard so much about, but John said *"I baptize you with water. But one more powerful than I will come, the thongs of whose sandals I am not worthy to untie. He will baptize you with the Holy Spirit and with fire"* (Luke 3:16).

Like John the Baptist, you can rise up and spread the Good News, but you have to be inspired. John was moved by the word of God. I was moved by the love of my grandmother.

Look deep within yourself and recognize what brings life and grace into your heart. It is this that can be shared with those around you. You are loved by God. This is an inspiration to love. You have read the Gospel. That is an inspiration to tell your friends about the Gospel. You have endured great suffering and learned wisdom. Teach others about suffering and wisdom. This is your calling.

Are You calling to me, Lord, are You calling? Is it my name or the just the sound of the empty wind that swirled around my heart? Oh, Lord, I am frightened.

Yes, You are calling me, Lord, and I answer. Oh, yes, Lord, I am no longer afraid.

Steps Toward Heaven

I will instruct you and teach you in the way you should go.
PSALM 32:8

It is true that when John the Baptist heard the word of God, he took up these words and began to preach. Remember what happened to Jesus when He was baptized as He came out of the water? *He saw heaven being torn open and the Spirit descending on him like a dove* (Mark 1:10). It is true.

I wonder if you have ever seen heaven being torn open? I wonder if I have ever seen such a thing. I believe that we have all seen things that point in that direction.

In the school where I work there is a bare spot in the floor at the door of the guidance office. This spot is located just at the point where a person opens the door to leave and places his or her foot at an angle to avoid being hit by the door when the door swings open.

I have often wondered how many people stepped on that spot in order for the floor tile to be so worn down as it was.

I have walked up the steps of the great churches of Paris and have seen the worn steps. Foot after foot simply moving up one step at a time. These steps are made of stone, yet the slight pressure of millions of human beings passing along that way cause the stairs to bow inward.

I think about the place where people spend a great deal of time walking. I think: *Others have been here, and so others will follow.*

I like to return to the house where I grew up and lie on my old bed. The room is the same. The windows are the same, but the boy is different. He has already traveled through this place, and someday there will be other boys hanging pictures of their favorite baseball teams on my walls.

As I was reading the *New York Times* one afternoon, I turned the page and was nearly knocked over by what I saw.

During World War II, the Allied Forces took many, many reconnaissance photographs of Europe in preparation for the invasion. Many of these photographs were never exposed. Apparently many of the films had been discovered. Someone going through the pictures came upon what was later discovered to be an aerial view of one of the concentration camps. It was a picture taken at a great height, but buildings, fences, and lines of people were clearly visible. It was determined that the line of people were standing before the wide doors of the crematorium. These people were standing in line for death. Step by step. Lord, have mercy.

Yes, when Jesus stepped out of the water, He saw heaven being torn open. I believe we are in the water of God's baptism, this earth and our lives. We are walking through our memories. We are stepping up to the fires of our tragic history. We are wearing down the steps of the churches, opening and closing doors, wearing down the floor tiles. We, the people, march on—reaching out for the ring of life: marriage, meals, children spraying each other with the garden hose on a hot August afternoon. We reach out for the ring of our being: love, months torn from the calendar, our wrinkled skin warm at the touch of our old, well-worked and loved hands.

We may not see heaven, but we see the direction, and if we follow the path that has been blazed before us by other men and women, by the apostles, by the risen Christ, well, it seems to me that we will, indeed, see the heaven Jesus saw before Him.

And remember, a voice came from heaven and said, *"You are my Son, whom I love; with you I am well pleased"* (Mark 1:11).

It's true! It's all true! *Start walking.*

I sing for the way, I call out for the way, I bow down in humble request for the way, my God, my Lord Jesus Christ. Point, push, lead, carry me on to the way toward heaven, for this day is the day that I wish to continue following You.

Look for God in the Person Beside You

Each one should retain the place in life that the Lord assigned to him and to which God has called him.

1 CORINTHIANS 7:17

During my eighteen-year career in education I have worked in five different school systems, under five different superintendents. The superintendent in a school is like the C.E.O. of a company. He or she is the boss who is held accountable by the board of education, again, much like any board that oversees a corporation.

A few years ago I was again in a new school system, once again about to meet my new boss. I made an appointment, arrived at the designated moment, and waited outside the superintendent's office. Not beyond being intimidated or impressed with people and their titles, I felt a bit nervous about meeting Dr. Winter. His door was closed, and his secretary sat behind her desk and smiled. "He'll be out in a second."

Was my tie crooked? Would I say the right things? Should I ask questions? The door opened, and a well-dressed man in a bow tie handed his secretary some papers, glanced up, and said, "Come on in."

I walked into the office and sat in one of two chairs that sat obediently in front of a large, glass-covered executive desk.

"I'm Bob Winter," the man said as he extended his hand and offered me a seat. Instead of walking around the desk, Dr. Winter sat in the other chair.

Was I to be official? Was I to speak about my ideas for the school district? How much of the man's time should I take?

"I read your book about your brother," Dr. Winter quietly began. "I was very moved with that book about Oliver."

I was startled. And then something even more startling happened. Dr. Winter and I talked and talked about my brother who was blind and crippled. Dr. Winter asked me about feeding Oliver, about how little intellect Oliver had. We talked and talked. Dr. Winter spoke about his childhood, about how difficult it is sometimes for him to express emotions and how much he liked what I had done in my book, speaking about things of the heart.

"I was able to hug my children all my life," Dr. Winter said. "I was capable of expressing my affection, but I was brought up in a household that was reserved. We were taught to hold back our emotions. I didn't want that for my own children."

We talked and we talked some more. After an hour, Dr. Winter was no longer my boss, my superintendent; he was Bob Winter, a man, a gracious, bright, open man who extended himself to his new employee.

I worked with Bob for nearly a year. I watched him in public meetings, in private meetings. I was in his office when he spoke on the phone. I listened to him as we shared lunch together numerous times in a restaurant. Again and again I saw Bob Winter acting not like a superintendent but like, well, Bob Winter.

In my first meeting with him I was able to know the man from the inside out. Most of the time we meet people, especially those with titles and position, from the outside in. Bob was the best superintendent I worked with. He was at a point in his career where he was hired by a bigger district and then, unfortunately, he was gone. But we have remained friends. We write letters, wish each other well. Bob taught me an important lesson: If you cannot be who you are in your worldly position, there is no point in being in that position at all.

How do we truly know a person? We can be lucky and meet people who, like Bob Winter, are willing to let themselves be quickly known.

John the Baptist acknowledged that he would have not recognized Christ if it hadn't been for the Spirit who had come down from heaven. *"I saw the Spirit come down from heaven as a dove and remain on him. I would not have known him, except that the one who sent me to baptize with water told me, 'The man on whom you see the Spirit come down and remain is he who will baptize with the Holy Spirit.' I have seen and I testify that this is the Son of God"* (John 1:32–34).

How often have you missed seeing Christ in the people you meet? How often have you judged a person just on his or her outward appearance and actions? Listen to what people say. Watch how they act. Notice words of compassion. Seek out deeds of kindness. These are like the doves from heaven, pointing out to you who are the ones blessed with inner grace and beauty. Most of us, by the way, *are* blessed with inner grace and beauty. It is our task, labor, and joy to find the deep insides of people so that we can love who they truly are.

When you sit in a bus or in a subway today, take notice of the people around you. See how distant they are. But have you ever seen, suddenly, a stranger smile kindly at you for some reason? Have you noticed how the stranger suddenly becomes familiar, for we recognize the smile of goodness?

Be open with the people you work with today. Be of good cheer. Do not play the false roles we believe we must act out. In the heart and mind of all you meet find the true person.

Teach me, Lord, to see Your face in each face of those I meet today. Help me hear Your voice in each voice I hear today. We know the Father by His children. Happy are we who live with the Lord.

Let Us All Go to Jesus

The kingdom of heaven is like treasure hidden in a field.
MATTHEW 13:44

Each summer, since I was a child, I have returned to a small town in Ontario, Canada, where my mother and father first visited in the late 1950s. They bought some property and built a small summer house.

It was in this town that I rode a horse for the first time, that I climbed into a hayloft for the first time. It was in this town that we took long walks to the small general store for ice-cream cones (chocolate for me). For two weeks in the summer, I was a country boy: rock hunting, swimming, eating wild raspberries.

We human beings like to return to those places that have brought us much joy. We like to be among familiar places. We like to be safe and happy.

After John the Baptist met Jesus, John returned the next day with two of his friends. And John said, *"Look, the Lamb of God!"*

When the two disciples heard him say this, they followed Jesus. Turning around, Jesus saw them following and asked, "What do you want?" (John 1:36–38).

John knew that he was in the presence of Jesus the day before, and he wanted to return the next day to the Man of Peace, the risen Lord.

After the births of our three children, Roe and I continued our visits to Canada with the children. I watch, each summer, as my son licks his chocolate ice-cream cone bought at the same general store. I watch our daughter climb up into the hayloft of the same barn where I whooped and laughed with my brothers and sisters more than thirty years ago. Our oldest son swims in the river, the same river I have always known. Is it the boy, or is it I, swimming in the afternoon sun?

We bring our children to the place of sun and water and hay and happy adventures. John the Baptist wanted to bring his friends to the Lord.

We are all missionaries, bringing the Good News to those who have not heard. My children would never have known about that river, that ice cream, those summers if Roe and I hadn't taken them there. How many people would never know about Jesus if it hadn't been for the Bible, our parents, a preacher, a neighbor, a friend?

"What do you want?" Jesus asked John and his disciples. Jesus asks us this question every morning that we awaken to. How do you answer the Lord? What do you want from Jesus?

For me, the answer is simple: I just want to be with You, Lord. It seems as if that is all John the Baptist wanted that day too. If we are with Jesus, we are forever in the water of life, in the sun of life, in the hayloft, laughing with our brothers and sisters.

John and his two friends *went and saw where he was staying, and spent that day with him* (John 1:39).

If we join Christ, we will surely see that our lifetime is one, single day of grace. Join the Lord. Invite your friends to meet Him. Do as Andrew, Simon Peter's brother, did. He invited his brother with these words: *"We have found the Messiah" (that is, the Christ). Then he brought Simon to Jesus* (John 1:41–42).

Let us all go to Jesus.

I see in the stars, in the rivers, I see in the open fields, patches of heaven and threads of paradise. Let me sew the earth, the day, the way of my life into a pattern that forms a quilt, God's quilt, to keep me warm today and always.

We Are All Part of God's Plan

Nazareth! Can anything good come from there?
JOHN 1:46

When we are up close to something, we sometimes have a difficult time understanding what we are really seeing. If we look at one grain of sand, can we really understand the entire summer beach? If we focus our telescopes on a single star, do we understand the universe?

Some scientists study the whole to understand the whole, while others study the single unit in order to understand the multiple considerations.

Walt Whitman embraced the notion that we human beings are part of a single soul, a single spirituality that is divided into the billions of people who have taken their small parts and connected them to a universal truth.

The poet William Carlos Williams, writing during the middle of this waning century, focused much of his writing on single stories: a woman stepping out from her house, a child playing in the street, a funeral, a birth. He observed the individual lives of those he tended to as a doctor and drew conclusions about their gestures, which were universal.

When I now look back at my brother Oliver, I begin to understand that both ways of looking at the world are valid. Oliver was blind and crippled. He didn't have an intellect. He could not learn, think, chew, walk, speak, embrace. For thirty-two years he was on his back in his bed. My mother and father, my brothers and sisters, and I bathed him, fed him, washed his clothes, and loved him. That is all.

My mother always said to us children that we had a saint in our house because Oliver never committed a sin. Who is sinless among us? I look back to Oliver's life, and I see a single person, in a single room. His presence in the house added a quality of peace that is difficult to explain. Perhaps it was like meeting someone in church who is praying and whom you do not wish to disturb. That type of peace. That type of presence. When I think of Oliver's peace, I think about all the possibilities for peace we are capable of in our own lives.

By feeding Oliver, my family was feeding all who are hungry. By bathing Oliver, we bathed all who are in need of cleansing. By adding an extra blanket over Oliver in winter, we comforted all who are in need of warmth. You see? By looking at a single person, we can look at the entire civilization.

Philip, one of the people Jesus met along the way as he decided to leave Galilee, *found Nathanael and told him, "We have found the one Moses wrote about in the Law, and about whom the prophets also wrote— Jesus of Nazareth, the son of Joseph."*

"Nazareth! Can anything good come from there?" Nathanael asked (John 1:45–46).

It is a wonderful question that Philip asked. Funny in a way, too, when we see what did indeed come from the town of Nazareth.

When Oliver was born, everyone felt the unanswerable question: Can anything good come from this severely retarded, handicapped, crippled, blind life? In a profound way my family and I had Nazareth in our home: up the stairs, second room on the right with the yellow wallpaper. Could anything of possible good come from that room?

Oliver taught us compassion, love, peace, courage. Tending to the weakest among us teaches us the power of true strength.

"Nazareth! Can anything good come from there?" Nathanael asked. "Come and see," said Philip (John 1:46).

When we were children and a new guest would arrive at the house, we so often said, "Want to see Oliver? Come, see."

Remember what Jesus said when He first met Nathanael? *"Here is a true Israelite, in whom there is nothing false"* (John 1:47). Oliver was like Nathanael. There was nothing false about my brother.

We all have our weaknesses, but remember, we all have our virtues too. You might ask yourself today, "Me? Can anything good come from there?" The answer is, especially in light of my brother's humble existence, "Of course, great goodness can come from you today, and that goodness swirling inside you is the way to Nazareth."

Jesus, because of You, the thimble of my heart is the ocean of love. Because of You, the grain in my eye is the earth's mystery. Because of You, Jesus, my single tear is the flood of happiness. Because of You, Jesus, my one breath is my entire life. You are the whole. I am the part. I raise my voice and thank You.

God's Flowers
Know When to Bloom

There is a time for everything, and a season for every activity under heaven.

ECCLESIASTES 3:1

Many years ago I was sitting in a public library doing research on children's television and literature. After I leafed through a few journals with disinterest, I pushed the publications aside and wrote this sentence: "If you think enough fanciful thoughts, something good is bound to happen." Following that line, I began to write on my pad of paper the start of a story about a girl who lived in the city with her father and with her cat. The girl's mother had recently died, and the girl felt a deep emptiness inside.

I sat in the library and wrote for two hours about the girl's home, about her backyard, and about her cat named Trab. I explained how the girl, Augusta, met her cat, Trab. And then I stopped writing. When I returned home, I explained to Roe what I had done. For the next six months I continued to write my little story. Finally it was finished.

During that time, the *Wall Street Journal* printed an essay I wrote about the importance of adults telling stories to children. An editor at a major New York publishing house wrote me a warm letter saying how much she had enjoyed the essay, and was I interested in writing children's books? I was not only interested, I wrote in reply, but I had just finished my story about the girl and her cat: *Augusta and Trab*. "Would you be interested?"

The editor wrote back saying that, indeed, she was interested. I wrapped the manuscript in brown paper, addressed the package, and sent it off to Manhattan.

I waited, and waited, and I waited for a response. Three weeks. Six weeks. Three months. Four months. Finally, I received the most puzzling rejection letter that ever arrived in my mailbox. The editor said that she liked the book but felt that the time wasn't right for me to be introduced to a wider reading public, so she was returning *Augusta and Trab*. I didn't understand. I understood only my disappointment. I opened the bottom drawer of my desk, slipped the manuscript under a pile of old, answered letters, and that is where the manuscript stayed for nine years.

I continued writing essays, which found their way into the *Reader's Digest,* the *New York Times,* the *Wall Street Journal.* I wrote and I wrote. One essay, the one about my brother Oliver, that appeared in the *Wall Street Journal,* led me to the writing of my first book, which led me to the writing of my second book.

With numerous articles and two books published, I opened my bottom drawer, pulled out *Augusta and Trab*, and mailed it to three or four publishers. A wonderful young editor-in-chief of Four Winds Press/Macmillan called to say that she could not imagine her life without having read *Augusta and Trab*. She loved the book, and so it was published.

This little book has brought me great joy. My children protect their copies with great care. One of the great satisfactions of being a writer is seeing my children reading and enjoying something I wrote. I know that they will someday read my book to their own children, and my grandchildren will read it to their children. On and on, perhaps.

My *Augusta and Trab* was not ready to be published when I first sent it out those nine years earlier.

All has its place in time. All will be as it ought to be in the universe. My closest friend, who lives in Pittsburgh, often says at the end of our phone conversations, "Chris, you know Who is in charge."

I believe the circumstances of our lives are guided by God and that we have free will to maneuver among the choices that are placed before us. I believe those choices are placed along the path we are destined to take. The choices are free, but the direction is guided. All we have to do is pray and to listen with our hearts.

When Jesus attended the wedding at Cana in Galilee, His mother came up to Him and said that there was no more wine. She knew that her Son could do extraordinary things. At first, Jesus said to His mother *"Dear woman, why do you involve me? My time has not yet come"* (John 2:4).

Jesus felt that it was not time to reveal His powers. But God must have felt that it was time, because Jesus, upon thinking about the situation, asked the servant to fill the empty stone jugs with water. When the water was served to the master of the house, the master was startled to taste such exquisite wine. It was time. The servants knew what Jesus had done. Can you imagine how amazed the servants must have been? Slowly, slowly, the Son of God was making Himself known. We are known by the actions we take.

Do you often feel it is not the best time to help your husband with a problem? Do you ever stop yourself and say, "It is not time to interfere with the problem at work"? Do you sometimes make plans and then realize that those plans ought to be put off for a while?

The buds seem to know the right time to bloom. Birds seem to know the right time to lay their eggs.

We are guided by an inner awareness of the correct moment to act upon our wills. Sometimes we don't know for sure, but then, suddenly, we are given hints of a direction.

If you are not sure about your plans at the moment, hold back until you feel that certain something that will clearly tell you to act. We often do not know why things happen or don't happen at the time we expect them to happen. But then a month, a year, twenty years later we discover the truth about the larger patterns of our lives.

The older we get, the more we understand how the different pieces of our lives fit together. Sometimes we try to fit a piece that can't fit yet because the other pieces haven't been created yet.

Be patient. The puzzle is forming. You will see the patterns. You will see the picture.

I am not deceived, Lord, by mechanical clocks. I do not allow the calendar on the wall to mock my age. Time is not locked between birth and death. You are the seasons. You are the ticking in my heart. You are the days. I cling to the pendulum of eternal hope and swing back and forth in Your arms, my Lord, and swing back and forth in Your arms.

God's Smile

Do not pay attention to every word people say.
ECCLESIASTES 7:21

It is unusual these days to see a man wearing a straw hat. It is unusual to see a man wearing a hat at all.

Often when I am driving through my little town in northern New Jersey, I see a certain man with white hair, winding his way through the streets, wearing a simple straw hat on his head, often carrying a newspaper under his arm as he walks.

One afternoon while I was standing in line at the bank, the man with the straw hat entered and stood in line behind me.

I turned around and said, "I've always admired your hat."

"What?" he asked.

"Your hat. I often notice you walking in town with your straw hat."

"What's the matter with my hat?" he asked in a cross voice.

"I just don't see many straw hats."

"Why not?"

"I think your hat looks nice, something old-fashioned."

"What about old? Did you say I'm old?"

I wasn't sure that I should have continued with my failing attempt at expressing my delight in seeing this man and his hat, so I tried to change the subject. "Nice weather."

"It's supposed to rain. My wife said to take my hat. It's made in Panama." He pulled the hat from his head, turned it upside down, and pointed to the label.

"It's a beautiful hat," I said.

"I hate it, but my wife makes me wear it, so I wear it to make her happy." Then the man with a straw hat offered for the first time a genuine smile.

It is difficult to see God in a grumpy old man until that man smiles and suddenly there is the light, the changed person, the true person revealed—the child of God.

Someone said to me once that we can see the features of God in a single smile. Look for that smile in the people you meet.

Now each time I drive by the man in the straw hat, I beep my horn. He turns, tips his hat in a quick gesture, smiles, and waves hello.

God of my smiles, remind me to laugh when I am happy; remind me to express joy when I am satisfied. Remind me, God, to rest in my happiness when I have done Your will. Keep me in Your heart that is laughing. Amen.

Inside Goodness

Therefore, if your whole body is full of light, and no part of it dark, it will be completely lighted, as when the light of a lamp shines on you.

LUKE 11:36

We were out, my family and I, selecting the best pumpkin we could find for our front steps. "This one," Karen decided. "It looks like the carriage in Cinderella."

As I carried the pumpkin to the car, Karen, who was six at the time, and her two brothers (ages four and eight) ran ahead of Roe and me. Autumn belongs to children dancing before their parents upon the brown fields of a new season.

"Can we carve the pumpkin?" David called out from the back seat of the car as we drove home.

"Can I help?" Michael asked.

"What can I do?" Karen wondered aloud.

"You can give the pumpkin his heart," I said.

"Yuck," was Karen's response.

After we pulled into the driveway, I lifted the pumpkin to my right shoulder as the children followed behind me into the house.

Roe spread a section of the *New York Times* on the kitchen table. David carried a knife over from the drawer. Michael asked if we could roast the seeds—"We did that in school." Karen was silent.

After I cut the wide cap from the pumpkin, we each took turns pulling the seeds, string, and goo out of the pumpkin's middle. Michael liked the goo. Then I began carving a face: two triangles for eyes, one triangle for the nose, and a crooked, nearly toothless smile.

Karen began to cry. "What about me?" She didn't like the goo or the seeds.

"Open the bottom drawer, Karen, and bring me the pumpkin's heart."

She stepped up to the drawer. "There's nothing here but a bunch of old candles."

"Yes," I said. "Please bring me one, Karen."

She brought me a white candle that I lit and placed deep into the belly of the pumpkin. Roe turned out the kitchen light. The children laughed as the dim candle reflected against their small faces.

"The pumpkin's heart," Karen whispered.

Yes, the pumpkin's heart, I thought as I sat beside Roe and the children.

What glows from the inside often reflects what is on the outside. Have you allowed the inside goodness of you to shine recently?

Do you sometimes keep yourself hidden from those you love? Are you afraid to reveal yourself sometimes out of fear or embarrassment? Those around you will notice the shadow and discomfort on your face.

Trust in God's love for you. Allow His light to illuminate your whole body, for when the eyes of those around you are focused on God's creation, your light will not be pushed aside by the shade. God's light will lead you to security and into the valley of the sun.

Carve a pumpkin this autumn. I am sure there is a heart to be lit somewhere in your house.

God of the sun, God of the stars, teach me how to collect the warmth of Your light that shines against my heart. Protect me from the shadow of evil. Protect me with the sword of Your light. Cut away the darkness. Today I am open for the radiance of Your power. Amen.

God and Suffering

Watch and pray so that you will not fall into temptation. The spirit is willing, but the body is weak.

MATTHEW 26:41

A friend of mine wrote speeches for the president of the United States. She invited me to lunch in Manhattan because she had read some of my work and liked what she saw. That is how we met.

I was nervous about meeting this bright woman. She was, after all, worldly, having spent many years in the White House, having traveled with the president, having written many books and articles.

I have spent most of my time in a small, white house in northern New Jersey, planting grass seed, washing the car, raising a family, and teaching in high school.

We met at my new friend's apartment. She invited me to roam freely as she finished getting ready. I saw pictures of her family, beautiful paintings, books, flowers. Her home was warm, comfortable, real.

We walked along the streets together and began sharing our different lives: her writing, my writing, her family, my family. In the restaurant, we spoke about authors we liked, books we'd read. Next, she began to speak about Thomas Merton and his book *The Seven Story Mountain*. She then started to speak about a feeling deep inside her. "I am looking for a strong, spiritual place in my heart."

The tall buildings of Manhattan surrounded us. Her career loomed large and successfully. In the face of her obvious talents and strength, she was speaking about God and fragility and Merton's difficult battle with God's calling. At that point I thought perhaps God doesn't really care about big buildings and success and fame and power. Perhaps He just wants us to love Him and to love one another. Perhaps all we human beings want is to be loved. Anyway, that is what I said to my new friend.

Then she asked me, "Why do people say that suffering is good for us?" I looked at her. She looked back at me. I said, "I don't know, but I do know that we are the only creatures on this earth who can ask that question."

My new friend wants me to write something about suffering. She is one of the most successful writers in America and she wants *me* to write about suffering? Thomas Merton has already written all she needs to understand about a search for God, about suffering, about the hidden joy waiting inside of us to be discovered.

Merton was a young man of lost dreams and a wild nature before he dedicated his life to God and to God's work as a Trappist monk. Because he was a womanizer, a sloth, a miserable person, he eventually drove himself into a deeply felt sense of suffering and emptiness. Finally, when Merton said yes to God, his suffering didn't go away. He turned away from foolish things and dived into the life of a spiritual adventure that was full of great suffering, but Merton discovered that suffering endured in the name of God is true gold compared to suffering in the name of self, which is stone.

Give yourself over to the risen Lord and you will feel your pain dissolve into wisdom.

In times of loneliness, in times of despair, in times of sickness, in times of doubt, we forget the Healer, we forget the prescription. I pray for all who are in need, for all who are ill. I pray for all those who suffer. I pray that they who feel pain will be blessed with a newfound cure: our Lord Jesus Christ in whom we have placed all our hearts and all our minds for solace and for redemption. Amen.

Love and Marriage

A wife of noble character who can find? She is worth far more than rubies. Her husband has full confidence in her and lacks nothing of value. She brings him good, not harm, all the days of her life.

PROVERBS 31:10–12

At a recent conference for school administrators I met a college friend I hadn't seen in more than twenty years. It is odd how we form close relationships during certain times of our lives, then, as we move on, we lose contact with these friends. It does place a question mark after the meaning of the word *friendship*.

At the coffee-and-roll table I shook this man's hand. We exchanged brief autobiographies: his children and wife, his career in education, the death of his parents.

I spoke about my wife and children and my career in education, then there was a request on the loudspeaker that all those attending the keynote speaker's address should report to ballroom six.

My old friend and I sat together in our dark suits. We listened to the speaker talk about the newest theories of education and management, then following the talk, there were questions, answers, a few final comments and it was over.

As my friend and I walked out of the room among the other people, he turned to me and said, "I'd like to tell you how I met my wife."

It seems that we can speak openly with a stranger. I hadn't seen this man in twenty years, and he had just said freely that he wanted to tell me a story. This puzzled me, but we returned to the coffee table.

"I was just out of college, visiting my parents. They had moved two years before from the house where I grew up. They said they didn't need such a big house anymore. They moved into a small house in Florida.

"My first night there I was restless. I opened the refrigerator and looked for a soda. My mother never bought soda, but I looked, just the same.

"My parents were sitting in the living room, reading. They spent most of their time together reading. She liked Tolstoy. He liked Proust.

"I called out from the kitchen, saying that I was going to the store for soda, then I stepped out into the humid Florida air. I walked about a mile toward the closest string of stores, thinking about the end of my college years, about the heat, about my parents reading back in a house I didn't recognize. As I walked into the milk store, I felt the immediate coolness of the air conditioner. I walked directly to the milk-and-soda case. I opened the long door with frosted glass and curled my hand around a single can of orange soda. I know this sounds silly, this exact memory, but that is what happened. The coolness in my hand, the heat of the air, my old parents. Then I walked to the front of the store. The cashier looked twenty. She noticed me and said, 'Real orange juice is better for you.'

"I looked at her smile. She rang up my purchase and placed the can in a plastic bag. I handed her a dollar bill, and she returned my change. I stepped out of the store, pulled the can out of the bag, snapped the tab, brought the soda to my lips. I sipped. I drank. I sipped again. I drank, then I walked back to my parents' house.

"Each night, for two weeks, I walked the mile, bought a single can of orange soda, sipped and drank, and felt the humidity against my skin.

"On the last night of my visit with my parents, I once again walked to the store. As I paid the cashier and as she returned my change, she whispered, 'Aren't you going to ask me out?'

"Five months later we were married. I never left Florida. We have five children. One died at birth, one is a freshman in Cornell. I have a son in high school. He wants to build houses. My two daughters, one married and one about to be, live in the same town. They see each other once a week.

"My wife and I spend a lot of time reading together. I still like orange soda, and the Florida air doesn't seem as humid to me as it once did."

After my friend shared this story with me, he emptied his cup of coffee in a last, single gulp, tossed the cup into a trash bin, shook my hand, and said good-night.

I haven't seen him since.

Recently, through another college friend, I learned that Jim's wife had died. I gave him a call. His voice was soft. "It was a terrible time. I do a lot of walking, and I am beginning to read Tolstoy."

Just as God has made a covenant with us, so we make a covenant with our husbands and wives: to love in sickness and in health, to pledge a holy union, to honor and to build a fidelity. Children imitate the parents. We children of God imitate the Father almighty who loves us in the fidelity of His union with us in the spirit. We are all married to God. We are all members of His wedding party.

Glory be to the faithful. Glory be to the children of God. Glory be to the husband and wife who live in the full joy of marriage. In matrimony we give thanks. In the memory of our vows we sing. Glory be to God. Amen.

The Stories Worth Telling

One thing I do know. I was blind but now I see!
JOHN 9:25

During my first year of teaching, one of my literature students called out, "Gee, Mr. de Vinck, you have really neat stories to tell." I stopped the class immediately and said: "Wait a minute. I'm not sure I like what you are saying. We all have stories to tell." The class looked at me.

"But all the stories you tell sound so great," said the boy. "I don't know. I wish I had neat things happening to me." What a sad thing for a boy who had marched through ten years of schooling to say.

One reason I became a teacher was to teach young people how to discover that they do, indeed, have neat things happening to them all the time. They just have to be taught how to *see*. For instance, let me tell you about a small incident that happened to me as a child many years ago.

My sisters and brothers and I were playing tag. During the game, we saw a snake that frightened us. We all ran home and drank Kool-Aid.

If we do not teach people how to refine their vision, they will simply look at events as I had just done. My snake story wasn't very interesting, I explained quickly, rushing through the experience with no reflection. Now, let me tell the story again but this time with a different vision.

Behind my neighbor's house there was a small brook, a wild meadow of tall grass, a few trees, and a swamp. One afternoon, my sisters and brothers and I marched across a small wood bridge. I can still hear the clomping of our feet as we crossed. (Sometimes, we pretended we were the goats in "Three Billy Goats Gruff.")

As we crossed over into the meadow, my oldest brother suggested that we play hide-and-seek in the tall grass, which was shaded by a single, young maple tree.

"Maria! You're 'it' first. Hide your eyes and count to fifty."

"One . . . Two . . ."

Four children scattered, laughed, and whispered. Two brothers ran to the edge of the meadow and sank into the grass. One sister ran in the opposite direction. I ran toward the maple tree; then I curled myself around the trunk, thinking that it was more difficult to be seen if I tried to blend in with the bark.

"Forty-eight! Forty-nine! Fifty! Ready or not, here I come." My sister broke away from her post and began searching.

One of the most serious times in a child's life is when he or she is hoping not to be caught in a game of hide-and-seek. I tried to hold my breath as Maria walked past me in her black-and-white sneakers. I remember hearing my own breath. As she passed, I wanted to laugh in victory, but I didn't. I watched her disappear into the grass. "Come on, you guys. I can't find you!"

That is when I began to look around: the grass before me, the soft earth beneath me. I turned my head and looked up into the branches of the small tree. There, two feet above my head, I saw a snaked curled around a *thin* branch.

"Snake!"

"Hey! That's not fair. You can't give yourself away!" Maria yelled out from across the meadow.

"Snake!" I yelled again. This time, everyone clearly understood the message, for there were four other children trailing behind me as we ran back across the bridge. *Clomp! Clomp! Clomp!*

We ran and we ran all the way home, up the side lawn, past the orange daylilies, under the rose trellis, up the stone steps, and onto the back porch.

"It was a snake! This close to my head! Up in the tree! I saw it!"

"Was it a python?" my little brother asked hopefully.

"I bet it was nothing but an old worm," Maria shrugged. "Let's go make some Kool-Aid"—which is what we did.

I will never forget how good that glass of red sugar water tasted, or how I felt sitting there in the safe kitchen with my brothers and sisters around me. One for all, and all for one. . . .

What lesson have you learned? A story is worth telling if there are little details and images: "wild grass," *Clomp! Clomp! Clomp!* "black-and-white sneakers," "orange daylilies," "red sugar water."

A story is worth telling if there is humor: "Was it a python?"

A story is worth telling if it is poignant: "the safe kitchen . . ."

Part of the responsibility of being a teacher is showing young people how to recognize what is beautiful, humorous, and poignant in their seemingly simplistic lives.

Jesus is our greatest teacher. Through the parables He taught us how to live. Through the "Our Father" He taught us how to pray. In His suffering and dying He taught us how to have faith in His guiding light. The substance of our lives is felt in the weight of what we consider important.

Do you think that Christ is important in your life? Can you feel His significance in your life today? The history of Christ is worth retelling. The reality of Christ is worth reliving each day.

I have listened to the Lord in all His telling; I have listened to the Lord define my life. I have listened to the Lord explain salvation. Sweet Lord, thank You for making me a character in Your book of life.

Precious Memories

"Peace, peace to those far and near," says the LORD.

ISAIAH 57:19

When we were children, my neighbor Albert and I created a song:

Pickles and alligators out on the lawn—
Who's gonna fight 'em before they're gone?

It all started when Albert's mother bought a jar of dill pickles. I had never eaten a dill pickle before. Albert called me into the kitchen and pointed to the counter. "Chrissy, look at the jar of baby alligators."

Everyone in the neighborhood knew that I had a dangerous imagination: dangerous to me. I believed anything I was told.

I couldn't understand why anyone would want to place alligators in a bottle, and I was even more disturbed that Albert's mother would buy such a thing in the market.

"Ah, that's not alligators," I said with much courage and authority. Eight-year-old boys know how to defend their notions with courage and authority.

"They are too!" Albert snickered.

"You old goat," I said and walked out of the house, onto the back porch, and down the stairs to the lawn. By the time I stepped on the grass, Albert was out on the porch, eating an alligator. He had another one in his right hand.

"Pickles and alligators out on the lawn!/Who's gonna fight 'em before they're gone?" Albert teased, then he threw the pickled alligator at me. It hit my shoulder and bounced onto the grass.

"That's no alligator," I said. "It looks like a cucumber."

Albert smiled, then took a crunching bite from his pickle. I picked up the pickle he had tossed at me and took a small nibble. I winced at the first taste, then I broke off another piece with my teeth and began chewing.

"Not bad," I said.

For years, whenever Albert and I began an argument, we'd end up chanting together:

> *Pickles and alligators out on the lawn—*
> *Who's gonna fight 'em before they're gone?*

After the publication of my third book, I received a letter from Paris. Albert had become a graphic designer for a French advertising firm. I hadn't heard from him in more than twenty years. He said that while browsing in an English bookstore he had stumbled across my book. This, in part, is what he wrote:

Dear Chris:

By chance I found your book this afternoon, and I felt compelled to write. Since I left the United States, I married, divorced, lost time, drew myself into an advertising position here in Paris. My ex-wife and our two children, boys, returned to America and are living somewhere in California, or so I imagine. Your book, *Only the Heart Knows How to Find Them: Precious Memories for a Faithless Time*, reminded me that I, too, had many good memories both in my adult world and in my time when we were young and throwing pickles at each other. I cherish my childhood memories, some of which included you and your brothers and sisters. I will not have the opportunity to watch my own two sons grow up, mostly because of my fault: infidelity and drinking, mostly. Jeannette (my wife) remarried. The last letter I received from her included a photograph of the boys and their adopted father out at a baseball stadium. I have terrible regrets but believe the children will be happier within a stable marriage.

Sometimes I wish I could go back in time and try to rearrange my life into a different pattern, but I am too closely tied to my selfishness and less sober ways that, at this point, I just accept my faults and have a difficult time dulling the pain. Your book helped.

Pickles and alligators out on the lawn—Who's gonna fight 'em before they're gone?

Sincerely,
Albert

Dostoyevsky, in his novel *The Brothers Karamazov*, wrote "There are no memories more precious than those of early childhood in one's first home." These memories sustain us as we grow older. Like God's promise at the time of our baptism, we are filled with important notions when we are young. In baptism we are blessed with the holy water of past and present acts of faith. We are anointed with God's promise that we will be saved. This symbol can protect us always, just as precious memories protect us and guide us in our times of loneliness or confusion or fear.

Why don't you think back today to some of your comfortable memories and think about the time God gently poured the cool water of salvation upon your forehead? These thoughts will brighten your day.

I remember the songs of my youth, I remember the sounds of many voices. I remember my schools and teachers. I will not forget the times of comfort. I will not forget the times of joy. And Lord God, I remember You from my past, embrace You today, and rejoice in the knowledge that You will still be there for me in the future. Amen.

Well-Seasoned Speech

You shall not misuse the name of the LORD your God, for the LORD will not hold anyone guiltless who misuses his name.
EXODUS 20:7

When I was a graduate student, living in the dorm, a friend of mine called on the telephone one afternoon and asked if I would mind taking care of his parrot for a few days while he flew west on a business trip.

"I'll be back in a week. All Sergeant needs is a banana, some oranges, and water."

After I agreed to take the bird, my friend arrived at the university a few hours later with Sergeant, a blue-and-red macaw parrot sitting on its perch in the middle of a brass cage.

"I brought some sunflower seeds too. You could cover his cage at night if you like. He doesn't need much else."

After my friend placed the cage on my bookshelf, we talked for a few moments about his trip, then he stepped to the doorway and pulled out seven bananas from a brown bag. "He's been fed for the day. He won't need anything until tomorrow morning."

"I'm sure we'll be fine," I said as I wished my friend good luck. "I'll see you in a week."

My friend was off, and I sat at my desk and began my studies for the evening.

At about eleven-thirty I was tired. I rolled out my paper from the typewriter, placed my work in a folder, stretched my arms above my head, closed my desk lamp, and walked over to the small refrigerator in the corner of my room in a hunt for a snack. The bird sat as still as stone in his cage and blinked a few times.

I ate a bowl of cereal, drank a glass of milk, flicked off the ceiling light, and walked to my room. It had been a long day.

It was easy to fall asleep quickly when I was younger. I didn't consider myself to be a writer. I wasn't married. I didn't have children. False dreams put me to sleep quickly. The dreams of my wife and children today cause me many difficult entries to sleep, not out of worry but out of joy, puzzlement, and wonder.

"Jesus Christ! Jesus Christ! Jesus Christ!"

It was one or two o'clock in the morning. I had been asleep for a number of hours.

"Jesus Christ!"

I was awakened with these two, distinctly pronounced words. I looked over at my clock radio. The time was illuminated in a foglike green.

"Jesus Christ!"

Again I heard the words, so I jumped out of bed and walked across my room, past my silent typewriter and the door. I snapped on the light, and there was Sergeant sitting in his cage, trying to pull a banana through the narrow bars of the cage. I hadn't realized that the bananas were sitting on the bookshelf within reach of the bird's claw.

Sergeant looked at me, then bobbed his head up and down a few times. I pried the banana out from between the bars, peeled back the skin, broke off a piece of the fruit, and handed it to Sergeant. He pulled it into the cage with his beak, held it in his claw, and began slowly eating the banana. I sat next to him, eating the other part of the banana. Sergeant and I in the middle of a Manhattan college dormitory. I was in my underwear. Sergeant shook his blue-and-red wings a bit.

I thought about Sergeant. He belonged in a tropical jungle somewhere, sitting up in a lush tree. I didn't know where I belonged.

"Jesus Christ," he said again.

I have read biographies of the saints, read the Old and New Testament. Many college professors spoke about God and the Greeks, the Orient and stars. I didn't expect the Good News to be delivered to me via Sergeant the parrot.

A few weeks after my friend returned from his trip and brought Sergeant home, he called me on the telephone.

"Chris, I'd like to thank you again for taking care of my parrot."

"Oh, that's okay. I enjoyed doing it."

"There's one thing, though," my friend said. "Now, whenever Sergeant is hungry, he calls out something that sounds like 'Alleluia'!"

Sergeant and I believed in responsorial hymns.

In Colossians 4:6 it is written, *Let your conversation be always full of grace.* Can you grace your spouse, child, colleague, or neighbor with a conversation filled with charm, goodness, honesty, and joy? When Christ asks us not to misuse His name, I believe He is asking us not to misuse the beauty of our speaking gifts. It is too easy to pepper our conversations with swearwords and vulgarities that detract from the music of our languages.

In the name of Jesus Christ try to speak with another human being today and listen carefully. See if you cannot hear how, the more you carry on the conversation, the more it sounds like a hymn.

Alleluia! Alleluia! Alleluia to the risen Lord. You are with me. You have kissed me. You have given me Your holy name. You have identified Yourself to me, O Lord, so that I may know You, so that I may follow You. I will protect our friendship. I will guard Your name. Thank You for the introduction. Alleluia.

Lending to the Lord

He who is kind to the poor lends to the LORD, and he will reward him for what he has done.

PROVERBS 19:17

Some years ago I was on my way home from a speech on my books in Syracuse, New York. My plane was due to depart at 8:15 in the evening. I arrived at the airport an hour before, checked in at the desk, bought a newspaper, and walked to Gate 12.

At each gate, comfortable chairs sat before the large picture window. I like to watch the jets move before me like giant whales in a holding tank.

As I began to read the paper, I glanced around and noticed three or four people waiting for the incoming plane.

Great, I thought. *Not many people. At least I'll have a peaceful flight home.*

I continued reading the newspaper. Ten minutes later I was distracted once again and turned my head to my left. I looked over my shoulder and saw, down the long hall, a mob slowly walking toward me: fathers, mothers, children carrying balloons, teenagers carrying radios and Walkmans.

Keep walking, keep walking, I said to myself. There were over a hundred people, *all going to Disney World,* I thought. *Keep walking.*

I tried to seem unconcerned as I smoothed out my paper and began to read another article. I peered over the edge of the newspaper just as a red balloon floated by me. To my right an old, old woman sat down with a long sigh. Behind me, a baby began to cry.

Within two minutes every seat, every space around me was filled with this tribe of nomads. *Where are the camels?* I laughed.

Were you ever caught in the middle of a drama?

I stood up and walked over to the courtesy desk and jokingly said to the woman, "Oh, well. Here I thought I had the entire plane to myself."

"Oh, they're not flying. They're waiting for passengers from the incoming flight."

At first I didn't think to ask who was receiving such a welcoming committee, so I simply began walking among the people who were, indeed, waiting. Finally I couldn't contain my curiosity. I edged my way closer and closer to a circle of five people. "Excuse me, but I just can't stop wondering. Whom are you waiting for?"

"Oh," said the woman with a pleasant voice, "our church is sponsoring a family from Armenia. The father came three years ago. We've finally been able to bring over his wife, his children, and his grandparents. We're here to welcome them. The family hasn't been together for three years. This is their last stop. Their new home. They've been flying from Armenia, to Rome, to New York, and now, finally, here to Syracuse."

This was much better than the newspaper, which I dumped into the trash can. Then I walked around a pillar among the large crowd as I tried to find a good spot to watch the reunion unfold.

Within ten minutes, a large jet rolled out of the darkness. Its nose nearly touched the glass window. The crowd was visibly moved with the impending drama. People stood up, adjusted their cameras, untangled the balloons.

Armenia. Earthquakes. Genocide.

The door opened. Passengers, obviously not from Armenia and obviously surprised with the crowd in the hallway, quickly stepped through. As each new passenger emerged from the closed doors, the anxious crowd took closer and closer looks.

Finally, as the doors were held back, someone called out, "I see them! Here they come!"

I stood on a chair and stared beyond the heads of everyone in front of me. And there they were: three children wrapped in bright wool coats and scarves, a young woman in a long black coat with a purple scarf wrapped around her head, and an old, old man walking arm-in-arm with an old, old woman.

I will never forget how the church people cheered and brought the young man before the crowd. I will never forget how the wife broke away from her children and embraced her husband. The teenagers reached over to the three Armenian children and tried to hand them the red balloons. The smallest girl cried. The old grandfather broke out in a toothless grin that should have been on the front cover of *Time* magazine.

The crowd cheered again and slowly walked together with the reunited family, down the carpeted hallway. Within minutes they were all gone, and all was as it had been before.

Those who are kind to the poor are actually giving to the Lord. The Bible says that God will reward them. After I witnessed the joy of this reunion, I wondered if God had not already rewarded everyone there.

Among our possessions, we can misplace the Lord. Lend to God today. Donate money or time to those who need it. You will be rewarded.

Lord of a thousand loaves and fish, may the coins in my hand jingle a song of hope as I share them with those who are in need. May the meal I prepare multiply as I feed those who are hungry. May the clothes I wear unfold to a multitude of clothes for those who are in need of warmth.

The Call of God

For many are invited, but few are chosen. . . .

MATTHEW 22:14

When I was a teenager, I was invited one summer to spend a month with my uncle and his family in southern France. During my first afternoon, as I walked through a cultivated field, I heard someone call out. At first I thought it was a voice of anger, for I had been trespassing, looking for a shortcut back to the cottage that my uncle had rented for the holiday.

The young man at the end of the field waved his hands back and forth, then I waved, too, realizing that he wasn't calling out in anger but in solicitude.

"Hello," he called out in perfect English. "Can you help me?"

I raised my hand again, then walked up to the man and shook his hand.

"What seems to be the problem?" I asked.

The teenager was equally puzzled that I, too, spoke perfect English.

"You're an American," he said more as a statement of fact than a question of interrogation.

"And you are British?" I answered with equal confidence. As I spoke, he stooped down and picked up some sort of an electrical device. There were dials, an antenna, and loose wires attached to a metal box.

"I'm visiting my uncle across the field. We're on vacation. I live just outside New York City."

"John Scott. I'm visiting my mother's family. They're out to the village. I'm flying my plane."

I looked around for a plane but saw none; then my new friend pointed up to a tree, and there, stuck in a high branch, hung a small model airplane of what looked liked a British Spitfire.

"I've been flying this all afternoon until it crashed up in this tree. I intended to climb the tree and rescue the thing but found myself without the proper courage." John Scott was on crutches. "I broke my leg in a boating accident a fortnight ago. Do you think you might fetch my plane?"

There was little need to explain, or to make a decision. The plane was an easy reach from the sixth or seventh branch, which was accessible to the other branches that formed a nearly perfect stepladder. When I lifted the plane up from its belly, John Scott applauded.

"That's a nickel's worth of valor," he laughed when I returned with his plane in my hand. "Will you have a bit of lunch?"

Lunch turned out to be a feast for the king's huntsman. John Scott hobbled to the end of the field, where a wicker basket waited for us. Chicken sandwiches. Pie. Wine. Pastries and bottled water.

"My mother prepared the meal, and my father drove me out against everyone's wishes—you know, a man on crutches, trying to fly a model airplane. All rather silly."

As I was about to finish my newfound meal, Scott turned to me and asked, "So what do you intend to do with your life?"

I was startled by the question, for no one had ever asked me such a thing, nor did I ask myself such a thing either.

127

"I don't know. I was thinking about becoming a teacher perhaps."

"No pay. Not much adventure," John Scott said as he drank the last of the wine and lifted the plane in his hands.

"And what are your plans?" I asked.

"I'm going to be a priest." John Scott looked at me, held his plane above his head, and made a roaring sound, imitating the plane's engine. "Would you hold the airplane as I set it off again?"

"Okay."

I wiped my mouth, savoring the last taste of apple pie, then I accepted the plane from John Scott as he began to adjust his black metal box.

"It's all electric," he said. "All you have to do is hold it above your head until I tell you to let it go."

I walked a few yards out into the field, holding the yellow plane above my head, when it suddenly jumped to life as the propeller began to spin and cut into the air.

"Hold it with the wind. Turn around!" Scott yelled. "With the wind!"

I turned and faced John Scott as he waved his hand, then yelled, "Start running, and then when I say so, let it fly."

I began to run. The engine coughed, spit, then kicked into its full power. I felt the plane tug against my hand.

"Let it fly! Let it fly!"

I released the airplane and watched it soar straight ahead. Then it took a quick turn upward and seemed to disappear into the light.

"That's the trick!" John Scott called out in triumph.

I stepped up to where he was directing the plane in its new flight. Over the roar of the distant plane I asked, "Why'd you want to be a priest?"

"My father wants me to go into politics, the ministry of some sort. My mother suggested engineering. My sister wants me to be a cowboy."

The plane zoomed higher and higher.

"But for the last year I've been watching my grandparents walk back and forth to the market each week. They walk arm in arm. She wears the shoes from the old century, those made of wood. He wears a tie that drapes in front of his coarse shirt. One afternoon, they returned with a bag of onions. I knew it was onions because I asked them later that day. I saw them walking through shadows of the trees. That is when I knew I wanted to be a priest."

"What's that got to do with wanting to be a priest?" I asked John Scott.

"I haven't the slightest idea. Something about walking through shadows, I think, and being old and carrying onions. They were expecting their grandchildren the next day, so they intended to make onion soup."

As John Scott and I were talking, we didn't take notice that the plane was flying farther and farther out of our range until Scott tossed the metal box into the woods. "Bother! There goes another one. That's the third plane I've lost. It'll fly for another half hour. Probably make it to the coast by that time. Come by tomorrow, and we'll fly a kite. They're much more reliable on the return trip."

I waved good-bye to John Scott as he hobbled down toward a waiting automobile.

That evening I told my uncle about my meeting the priest-to-be in the field beyond the hedgerow.

"Oh, him," my uncle said. "He's nothing. Plans to be some sort of engineer or something. Always fiddling with gadgets."

Years later I received a letter from England, from a Father John Scott. He had read one of my books and wished to tell me so. He ended his letter with these words:

"Chris, you were the first one I ever told about my wishes to pursue what God guided me to do. I wanted to be an engineer and design airplanes, but that onion soup was the most delicious I've ever tasted."

The call from God in our lives comes in different ways but always with power. *Our gospel came to you not simply with words, but also with power, with the Holy Spirit and with deep conviction* (1 Thessalonians 1:5).

What is God calling you to do for today? And for tomorrow? And for the rest of your life?

Lord, the power of Your will is close at hand. Help me understand how I can reach out and answer Your call. Fill me with wisdom so that I may not be diverted. I wish, my Lord, to follow You.

Pointing to the Promised Land

Therefore go and make disciples of all nations.
MATTHEW 28:19

I will tell you one of the reasons I became a teacher. Perhaps this may give you a reminder to look at your own life to see how you came to be the person you are today.

In looking back over our lives we can see the patterns that have been formed for our living. The questions we should ask are these: Are the patterns accidents? Were these patterns of our life placed before us as a guide?

After I read the novel *The Grapes of Wrath* by John Steinbeck, I knew that I wanted to be an English teacher. I was a junior in high school. I knew that I liked people, and I knew that I liked to read. When I read about the Joad family and about Rose-of-Sharon's compassion at the end of the novel, how she offered her own breastful of milk to a starving old man even though her own baby had recently died—when I read these things, I knew that there was more to books and to life than I had known before, and I wanted to be a part of this something new.

It was my goal as a teacher to teach my students to embrace the people they read about as if these people were sitting beside them in the classroom.

It was my joy to take my students on journeys into the hearts and minds of people who clearly lived in courage, with dignity, in faith.

Steinbeck's bedraggled family lumbered across America in search of the promised land. The promise was fulfilled in their own souls, not in the fertile farm land of California.

That is what gave me a notion about becoming a teacher, a discovery that there is a promised land: home, family, goodness. This is the discovery that I can share with young people.

A student stepped up to my desk one afternoon at the end of the year and said, "Mr. de Vinck, I think I'd like to be a teacher."

"Why?" I asked the young man.

"I can't explain it exactly. Something in the books we read this year, I think."

I understood.

The next time you meet some high school students, tell them how you started your career. Tell them about the patterns of your life and how they lead you to courage, dignity, humor, and faith. Especially faith. Young people will listen.

I pray for the youth of the world. I pray that they may gather the seeds of faith for their own children, and for their children's children, for then we can say that we have taught them well. For this I pray.

Hidden Acts of Kindness

Always try to be kind to each other and to everyone else.
1 THESSALONIANS 5:15

I heard a story this afternoon that illustrates the power of the generous act. This story is about a friend who owns a small, red British sports car, the famous Triumph. Apparently this man keeps this car in perfect condition. At the slightest hint of rust, he brings out his paints, sandpaper, and patch tools and works the metal to its original luster. He keeps the machine tuned and oiled, and he drives the car only on weekends and in good weather.

One afternoon he received a call from his daughter that she needed to be picked up from a friend's house after a roller-skating party.

On that particular day, the man's wife was out shopping. The other car was in the repair shop for new brakes. The only car available was the red Triumph.

The father looked out the window as he was speaking with his daughter on the phone. The clouds were dark, but the man said he would come right away. He hung up the phone, walked to his garage, stepped into the sports car, and drove to the skating rink.

Because it was a warm afternoon and because the clouds didn't seem to be doing anything, the man decided that he would drive with the top down after all.

Following a fifteen-minute drive, the father reached the rink, parked the red sports car, and walked under the large, neon sign: "Skater's World." Once inside, the man was greeted by other parents retrieving their sons and daughters. All the young people, including the man's daughter, wanted to stay just a few more minutes.

A few more minutes extended to a half hour. Loud music echoed throughout the rink as people skated around and around and around until finally the DJ announced that the afternoon session was over.

When the microphones were switched off and the music died, the father and everyone else in the skating rink heard the loud thunderstorm in progress. The man suddenly remembered his Triumph sitting in the parking lot with its top down. He hurried his daughter as she unlaced her skates and shoved her feet into her shoes. The girl quickly said thank-you and good-bye to her friends and ran to keep up with her father, who was already halfway down the main hall of the skating rink. The daughter ran and ran, then she stopped for she saw that her father was standing outside the main door, looking across the parking lot.

"What do you know about that," the father said to his daughter.

"What is it, Dad?" she asked.

"Mom was out shopping, and the other car is in the garage, so I had to take the Triumph."

"The Triumph? In the rain?" the daughter gasped.

"With the top down," the father smiled.

"Dad. How can you smile? You protect that car as if it were a baby!"

"Look," the father pointed.

Sitting in the parking lot in the heavy rain, sat the red sports car with its top down. But there was also something more. Someone had placed a large piece of plywood over the entire car, and all the rainwater had never touched the uncovered, exposed automobile.

Acts of kindness, especially anonymous acts of kindness, are true gifts not only to the receiver but also to the giver. Can you imagine the pleasure the person must have felt when he ran through the rain with the plywood to protect the stranger's car?

See if you can create an anonymous gift of kindness to someone today. Perhaps you could send a small note of encouragement to someone in your office? Send flowers to a neighbor who is lonely. Place a basket of fruit on a friend's porch.

Can you imagine all the acts of kindness God does for you each day without your even realizing it?

I found the sun for me this morning. I thank You, Lord. I found the warm water in the shower. I praise You. I found the bread in my kitchen this morning, Lord. I thank You. I found the fresh air as I stood out the door. I praise You. For all that I see that You do for me, I thank You. For all that I do not see that You do for me, I praise You.

A Woman of Dignity and Hope

Pursue righteousness, godliness, faith, love, endurance and gentleness.

1 TIMOTHY 6:11

We never know what lasting impression we make in the world. We cannot guess that by our living we influence those around us in ways that we will never realize. Ruth is a good example.

I met Ruth when I was a teenager during a summer vacation in Canada. In a conversation with this woman I learned that she lived in the next town from my parents' home in New Jersey. This was the first time I realized how small the world is, meeting someone from New Jersey in a remote little town in the heart of Ontario.

My parents met Ruth, and then she established a long friendship with my family. Ruth loved the color lavender. Her clothes were lavender. Her shoes were lavender. Her car was lavender. Ruth was a schoolteacher. She lived alone a few hundred feet from the highway in a small, gray house that was neat, clean, filled with lace, straw flowers, colonial furniture. Simple, warm, and ordinary.

Eight years after they were married, Ruth's husband died. Her two sons were born with severe mental disabilities to such a degree that they both had to be institutionalized. Ruth died of cancer.

I remember one afternoon when she called on the phone and asked if I would like to stop by and rake her leaves. As an unemployed teenager, I was eager to pick up any extra pocket money. I drove to her house. She was waiting for me sitting on her front step, with a rake in her hand.

"Hello, Christopher," she said as she stood up. I remember how difficult it was for her to walk. She smiled with a joke, "My bones were put in backward."

Ruth handed me the rake, then swept her right arm out over the garden. "All the leaves, if you could. And inside the bushes. You can rake them in a pile onto the road. The town will pick them up next week." Then she once again passed her hand over the land before us as if she was giving the land a blessing. "I planted this lawn. Grass is a crop, you know," Ruth said, "just like farming. My father had a farm: beans, corn, and out the distant way, apples and pears."

Ruth walked inside her little gray house, and I spent the afternoon raking. As the sun was about to give up its day's watch, Ruth called from the front door, "Christopher, that's fine, just fine. Come in for some cake."

As I pulled the last leaves from under the last bush, I smelled the evening air settling in around me.

"Sit there." Ruth pointed to the chair at the head of her oak dining room table. She sat at the other end after she placed a piece of pound cake on a plate and handed it to me.

As I ate my cake, I looked at Ruth in her lavender shawl. She must have once been beautiful. On the wall behind her hung a single picture of a young man in what looked like a banker's suit: stiff, white collar, dark tie, clean, straight. He was standing beside a tree.

"Would you like another piece?" Ruth asked.

I was about to say no, thank you, but Ruth had already cut the cake and was reaching out for my empty plate.

At Ruth's funeral, six months later, in the eulogy the priest spoke about Ruth's teaching career, about her husband and children, and then he said, "Many people do not know why Ruth loved lavender so much. She told me that when she first met her husband, he sang that silly tune to her one evening on the way home from the movies: 'Lavender's blue, dilly, dilly,/Lavender's green;/When I am king, dilly dilly,/You shall be queen.' That was the night he proposed to her."

Our reign as kings and queens can be spent lording over great territories and ruling thousands of people, or it can be a simple, quiet time tending to a small piece of ground, a yard, a field.

As you go about your routine today, think of yourself as a grand lord or lady. Consider your land and subjects. Lift up your arms, wave them back and forth, and say in your heart, "This is good." Dilly, dilly.

The space I occupy, Lord, is where You have placed me. I pray that I may be worthy of Your will. Help me see the vastness in my small surroundings. Help me see the beauty. Through Your intercession I have found my garden where I may grow and praise You.

God of the Dance

Let them praise his name with dancing.
PSALM 149:3

Here I am afraid of the dance, incapable of dancing, believing in the possibility of the dance and yet put off by the image of my clumsy body and self-consciousness moving to the rhythms of the music from the distant stage.

When I was a boy, I liked to pretend that the woods behind my house was the place for adventure. Trees were ogres. Certain rocks taller than I were bloated dragons that I defeated with empty bottles I'd throw from a distance until I heard the comforting crash of shattered glass.

Once I imagined that I danced with a crow. I didn't think of this crow as a dancing partner when I first saw its crumpled body at the northeastern section of the woods. When I stooped down to investigate, I quickly saw ants crawling inside the dried eye-socket of the bird. I grabbed a stick and poked what remained of the bird, for I thought perhaps it wasn't finally dead. There was no magical cure in my stick, so I threw it over the fence of the neighbor's property.

I stooped down once again to admire the crow's black feathers. I wanted to pluck some of the feathers and bring them to my mother, for she had a collection of feathers in a clay pot on her dresser in her bedroom. Her grandest prize was a pheasant feather she had found one spring on the back lawn.

I was about to pull the feathers from the wing, but then I was afraid. Would the bird bleed? If it was still alive, wouldn't it hurt to have its feathers yanked out? Did the feathers have a disease? I regained my courage and grabbed the tip of one wing and pulled. Instead of freeing up a feather, I was able to extend the crow's entire right wing. Then I grabbed the tip of the left wing and exerted the same amount of pull I had used on the right wing, and sure enough, I was able to extend the left wing as well. I stood on the ground. The dead bird was stiff and attached to the hungry earth, but the two wings were stretched out before me like spring ferns or Japanese fans. I held the wings out extended before me; then I felt ants crawling on my bare arms. I released the powerless wings, turned, and ran home.

Many years later, at a high school dance, I was interested in a particular girl who knew my name and shared a lab table with me in biology. As the evening progressed, I was more and more determined to ask this girl to dance. She was bright, popular, confident. I didn't even know how to make a proper knot in my necktie, but boys take risks, and youth is driven by ignorance.

I walked up to the girl just before the band played another song. "Want to dance?" I asked.

She looked at me and asked if I had finished the biology homework.

"Well, no," I said as I looked at her pale arms hanging down from her shoulders.

"We're supposed to use color pencils for the circulatory system." We were studying rats, and Mr. Berry had given us a ditto to color and label in preparation for the next week's dissection class.

The band played a slow, peaceful song. "Would you like to dance?" I asked again weakly.

"Yeah. Sure."

My father was a ballroom dancer in his youth. No one in high school danced the waltz. I didn't know how to dance in any form or in any fashion. The girl was obviously perplexed when I grabbed her left hand in my left hand and when I grabbed her right hand into my right hand. She looked over at her friends. Was I supposed to pull her close to me? Were we supposed to sway back and forth to the music? I realized that many people were watching us. I remembered that dancing had something to do with feet, so I risked a few steps backward then forward. In my sudden frustration, I just stood still. Then I lifted her right arm into the air, and then I lifted her left arm. Someone laughed. My hands were sweating.

When the song was over, I dropped the girl's arms. "See you in biology," she said with a strained smile as she returned to her circle of friends.

In a Greek myth, Icarus, son of Daedalus, was able to fly using the grand wings that his father had created with feathers and wax. The young man's powerful arms lifted him higher and higher and, against the caution of the father, the son flew too close to the sun, which melted the wax, causing the feathers to detach from his arms, and Icarus plunged to his death into the raging sea.

As I walked home in the dark the evening of the dance, I remembered the crow's wings and how they, too, extended before me in a different sort of dance. What if I had plucked those feathers, after all, and placed them in my hair and flapped my arms through the woods and up the lawn to where my mother sat on the porch reading the *New Yorker* magazine?

What if I had taken that girl into my arms and waltzed her through the crowd, out the door, and up to the moon and back?

Most of us do not dare disturb the universe, as T. S. Eliot wrote. We cower at convention, succumb to our fears, risk little, dream less.

I have learned as an adult that I'd rather be Icarus flying toward the sun than be the one sending the girl back to her unkind crowd, and I am sorry that I abandoned the crow to the hasty ants.

I believe we all have a dancer hidden inside of us. Do you sometimes feel inhibited? Do you feel sometimes that you act the way people expect you to act instead of acting the way you *want* to act? Why not take a risk today and do something a little crazy: Sing a song at the breakfast table, or go horseback riding, or change the color of your house, or wear flowers in your hair all day?

Whatever you do, change, take a risk, and above all else, laugh. I think God likes it when we laugh.

I dance to the music, and I dance to the silence. I dance to the risen sun, and I dance to the evening moon. I dance, and I dance because I am a child of God.

Look Homeward, Angel

Return home, my daughters.

RUTH 1:11

When I worked in New York City, I often walked passed the Empire State Building. Each time, I pulled my head back and traced the height of the immense structure with my eyes.

I once heard that the man who designed the building was sitting at his desk, contemplating what this new project ought to look like. As he sat considering the challenge, he tapped his long, yellow pencil on the desk. As the architect thought and thought, he continued fiddling with the pencil until he stood the pencil up straight on its eraser and there, suddenly, the man saw the idea for the new construction: the shape of a pencil.

I do not know if this is a true story, but the Empire State Building does look like a giant pencil standing up straight in mid-Manhattan.

How do we fit between the buildings of a city that loom over us? Where is our place in the world?

One day during the last month of my work in New York, I decided that on my lunch break I would ride the elevator to the top of the Empire State Building.

After paying my fee, after stepping into the elevator, I thought about my grandparents and how, when I was ten, they dragged my brothers and sisters and me to the top of the building. It was in the cold spring. I remember seeing my grandmother pointing and gazing out toward the ocean as we stood on the observation platform. "From there is where we come," she said.

I squinted my eyes and tried to see the Belgian coastline that I was sure would be visible on such a clear day.

During my second visit to the top of the world, I was alone. Well, I wasn't physically alone, for there were many tourists in the elevator and many more walking around the observation deck. But I was alone *inside*.

I walked around the top of the building, looked up at the large television-and-radio antenna. I looked out across the Hudson River and tried to locate the hills of my hometown in New Jersey. I looked down into valleys of the city and followed the miniature cars that moved through the small streets.

I turned and looked out toward the ocean. I squinted my eyes and tried to see Belgium again, but no luck. As I stood in the cold, a woman standing next to me asked, in a British accent, if I had change. She wanted to look through the rent-for-a-quarter binoculars. I gave her four quarters for a dollar. She seemed to be my age, in her early thirties. As she fed a single coin into the dark slot of the machine, she said, "I've never been up here before."

I thought the money exchange was the end of our relationship, but then I said, "This is my second visit."

"Yes? When was the first?" the woman asked as she swung the binoculars to the right, out toward New Jersey.

"When I was ten. I came up here with my grandparents."

"My grandfather helped construct this building," the woman said as she gave the deck a solid thump with her right leg. "He also regularly beat my grandmother, and she finally left him."

I was startled with this sudden intimacy. "Where did she go?" I asked, not sure what to say.

"Hoboken," the woman said as she adjusted the focus on the binoculars. "Over there," she pointed across the river. "I'm here just overnight from England. I wanted to take a look at New Jersey. That's where my mother was born, alone with my grandmother. She grew up in Hoboken."

The timer in the binocular machine clicked shut and the eyepieces closed. The woman looked at me and smiled. "I just wanted to see Hoboken before I flew back to England. Thanks for the change."

The woman smiled again, placed her hand on my arm, walked to the elevator, stepped inside, and disappeared.

I stayed on the observation deck for another half hour. I looked down at the distant streets and watched people walk along the sidewalks, cross the avenues, enter buildings. A jet plane flew over the city. Cars swirled around and around. A brown barge moved slowly upriver. As I stood on the near tip of the pencil point of the Empire State Building, I thought about the grandmother in Hoboken. I thought about the granddaughter flying home to England. I thought about my grandmother buried in Brussels.

Each life is tied to a story, a place, an inconvenience, a labor, a sudden realization that Hoboken is a myth, a place that no longer hurts, a time long ago when our grandparents were young—hoisting girders, making love, starting out to end in broken promises, victories, or defeats. Time may pass suddenly in a given life, but we remember from where we come. Oh, to grab the tall pencil and scratch into the sky the name of my grandmother!

I dropped a quarter into the binocular machine, spun it around and, as I stood perfectly still, I thought I could barely see the slight traces of the Belgian coastline.

We all belong to another world, to another time, to another place of long ago. I believe it is important to share your history with those you love so that they will be able to tell their children about the foundation of their lives.

Is there a story about yourself you haven't told your family? Perhaps tonight, at the dinner table, tell them. Share a part of yourself in this new way. The more we know the people we love, the more we can love them.

From the time of my birth to the time of my childhood, to the time of my adolescence, to the time of my youth and middle age, to the time of my old age, I am the same person, Lord—Your servant, Your creation, Your child. Take my hand today and lead me around the park of my life as You and I consider the angels flying, flying, flying, Lord God the Father.

Praise God For Our Lives

Praise be to the God and Father of our Lord Jesus Christ! In his great mercy he has given us new birth into a living hope through the resurrection of Jesus Christ from the dead, and into an inheritance that can never perish, spoil or fade—kept in heaven for you, who through faith are shielded by God's power until the coming of the salvation that is ready to be revealed in the last time.

1 PETER 1:3–5

Today, March 31, is Michael's birthday. Michael, my son. At the time that I write this, he is ten years old. When I turned ten years old, my grandfather looked down at me with a wise grin and stated, "Christopher, this will be the best year of your life." Even then I felt that was a sentence of doom. What about the rest of the sixty, seventy, or eighty years?

Michael was born at four in the morning. By the time Roe and I arrived at the hospital, all seemed ready, including Michael.

Because the customs and rules had finally been relaxed, I was able to be in the birthing room with Roe, which was specially decorated with curtains, colorful walls, bedspreads. The idea was to make the room look as much like home as possible. Of course, during labor, everyone involved would not have cared if we were on a city street.

At the time of delivery, Roe looked at me, and then she asked, "Are you all right?" She was having the baby, and I was fainting. But the nurse gave me some orange juice, and the doctor said, "Come, look, Christopher!" And there was Michael. Born. Crying. Little.

When we brought him home, he was an immediate star. His older brother and sister thought he was funny and cute. Everyone wanted to hold him.

I still carry Michael up to bed on my back. He still likes to pretend that I am his horse as he pulls to the left or right and I respond with a whinny. Sometimes he is so tired he just leans against my back, carrying the blanket his aunt made for him when he was born.

Michael is bright, charming, full of fun, athletic. He reads, and he plays hide-and-seek with our dog Keesha.

Michael and I run around the house, chasing each other with Nerf crossbows, play catch in the yard, drive to town for an ice-cream cone. Michael is what children should be: happy, confident, brave, funny, pesky, loud, innocent, grateful, generous.

Last night, as I was tucking Karen in bed, I heard Michael suddenly laugh aloud in his bedroom with much vigor and commitment. After Karen kissed me good-night, I walked into Michael's room and asked him what was so funny.

"Look at this, Dad," he said as he turned back a few pages to a Jim Davis *Garfield* book. There was Garfield in another one of his funny, sarcastic moods, and Michael laughed aloud again just from looking at the cartoon.

I leaned over and kissed him good-night. "In three hours you will be ten years old."

He looked at the clock: 9:00. "No I won't, Dad. I'll be ten in . . . seven hours. Remember, I was born at four in the morning."

"Yes, that is true. You were born at four. In seven hours you will be ten years old. Michael, every day you have been a joy to Mommy and me."

"I know. I know. You love me."

Michael kissed me good-night, read in his *Garfield* book for another ten minutes, clicked off his lights, and slept.

For his birthday today he received a sticky plastic bug that crawls down smooth surfaces, a video game, Goofy slippers, eight rocks for his rock collection, underwater Legos and, carved from wood, a beautiful model sailboat that really works.

In the evening, Michael was in the basement with four of his friends for a birthday sleep over. Before running down for the night, he slipped into my room where I was writing and whispered, "I love you, Daddy. Thanks for the presents," then he kissed me good-night.

"Good-night, my boy. I love you, and I am very proud of you. This is just the beginning of many, many wonderful years to come." He grinned and pointed to the wall behind me. There, crawling slowly down the wall, was a red-and-black, sticky plastic beetle. Michael laughed and laughed when I pretended to be frightened.

Today is also my father's birthday. He is eighty-three years old.

God knew what He was doing when He created us all. Birthdays ought to be celebrated. Think about all we do for Christmas in order to celebrate the birth of Christ. We are people of celebration. We celebrate the New Year, a new job, a success, a new house. It is only fitting that we celebrate the birth of a new person.

Perhaps people you love are celebrating their birthdays today? Call them on the phone and offer them your love, then hang up the phone and say a small prayer of thanksgiving to God for the birth of these important people in your life.

Though I have seen the oceans and mountains, though I have read great books and seen great works of art, though I have heard symphonies and tasted the best wines and foods, there is nothing greater or more beautiful than those people I love. Thank You, dear God.

In Words We Find Truth

This is what we speak, not in words taught us by human wisdom but in words taught by the Spirit, expressing spiritual truths in spiritual words.

1 CORINTHIANS 2:13

One spring evening when I was a boy of twelve, I heard the garbage can crash to the driveway gravel. I stood up from my chair, walked through the living room, through the dining room, and brushed back the window curtain. Through the thin darkness a round, small figure wiggled out from the garbage can, dragging a plastic bag filled with apple peels. As I tapped my right index finger against the window, the raccoon swung up from the bag, turned its head slightly from side to side, returned to its labor, picked the bag up into its mouth, and ran toward the woods.

A few nights later, I heard the trash barrel once again fall to its side. This time, I ran through the kitchen, grabbed a flashlight, and crept down to the basement. The north window faced the garbage cans. The flashlight beam caught the raccoon in the act of licking the juice from an empty can of fruit cocktail.

As a child, I had an affection for animals to such a degree that all the neighborhood children knew that if they found a stray cat, an abandoned bird, or a lost giraffe, for that matter, they could bring it to me and I would nurse it back to health or find it a home. I raised a robin, a squirrel, a possum, a starling, a skunk, sixteen rabbits, and a moth.

Each week during the time of the raccoon, when the garbage can rolled on its side, I ran down to the basement window to observe this creature from the deep woods.

One evening, as I ran through the kitchen on the way to my rendezvous with the raccoon, I grabbed a bunch of grapes from the refrigerator. By the time I reached my observation post, the raccoon had already gutted the trash can. Ripped bags, empty cans, eggshells, orange peels decorated the driveway with little artistic symmetry.

Then I had an idea. I reached over, turned the lock at the top of the window, and slowly lifted the window to its full opening. I thought that the raccoon would run. It looked at me, smiled, perhaps, and returned to its investigation.

I knew that raccoons savored fruit, so I picked a grape from the stem I had brought from the kitchen and threw it at the feet of the portly intruder. The raccoon turned its nose down to the grape, picked it up, rolled it around a bit in its paws, then jammed the grape into its mouth.

I tossed another grape, and once again the raccoon picked it up, washed it, and quickly devoured it in a single sweep of its teeth.

I was about to leave when I noticed the raccoon looking in my direction, then slowly walking toward me. "Hello," I said. The raccoon stopped, looked toward the woods, then continued to step closer and closer. I picked another grape from the stem and tossed it at the oncoming creature. It stopped, ate the grape, then continued toward me. "Well, hello," I said again, waving the grapes back and forth.

I stepped back into the basement and tossed another grape out onto the ground. A moment later, a small, dark paw extended into the basement. I reached over and placed a single grape into the paw. The raccoon curled its small claws around the grape and retracted its paw. A few seconds later the paw once again entered the basement. I was about to pull another grape from the stem when the raccoon reached in even farther and grabbed the entire bunch of grapes from my hand.

By the time I reached the window, the raccoon was already halfway to the entrance to the woods. It turned once in my direction, perhaps to say thank-you.

A few days later I sat on the edge of the bathtub while my mother soaked her hair and curlers with a hair-permanent solution. I liked to be next to my mother when she baked, arranged flowers from the garden, read magazines. We lean against those we love, are nurtured by the circle of their presence.

"Mom," I said while she squeezed a plastic bottle of liquid onto her hair, "I'd like to read a book."

I never asked my mother or father or anyone for a book to read. To this day I do not know what provoked me to ask such a question. My life before that time was consumed with the garden, the woods, the swamp, Davey Crocket, raccoons, brothers and sisters, grass huts, tree forts, swimming, skating.

"I'd like to read a book."

My mother grabbed a towel, wiped her face, turned to me, and said, "I'll see what I can do."

A few days later, in the last evening hours, I walked up the stairs tired and prepared to sleep. I flicked on the lights, undressed, and ... there, something was on my pillow. A book. My mother had surprised me with a book. I jumped onto my bed and lay flat on my stomach. I looked at the cover and there, in a black-and-white illustration, was a boy about my age and his raccoon, Rascal. I began to read the book and I read and I read. In three days I had finished the book. It was the first book I had read in my twelve years. I was taught how to read, but schools in those days didn't nurture a reading habit. Children weren't expected to read whole books in a school curriculum, and there was no notion that children ought to read novels.

By the luck of circumstances and my mother's insight, I was connected, for the first time, to a book. *Rascal* changed my life, though I didn't know it at the time.

There has been wonderful research that has discovered that fifth-grade children who do not like to read are exposed to about 10,000 written words a year. Children in fifth grade who love to read and read often are exposed to about 4.6 million words a year. Guess which children have better vocabularies, writing skills, reading skills, thinking skills? Obviously, the children who read 4.6 million words a year.

I spent many, many summer nights feeding the raccoons out from the basement window. I was able to feed them by hand, take photographs of them, pick up the baby raccoons, and pet their soft coats. Little did they know that they were partly responsible for introducing me to books and to an eventual career as a writer.

The next time a raccoon spills your garbage can, send it off with a few grapes and say thank-you for me.

One of the very best things you can do today for your child or grandchild is to buy him or her a book. As Jesus is our teacher, we, too, can bring light into the lives of the children we love with books, books, and more books.

I pray for the children, for the words of God to enter into their hearts, for the words of hope to enter their minds, for the words of charity to enter their deeds. Bring, my Lord, the gift of reading into the lives of all children.

The Soul Knows

Praise the LORD, O my soul.

PSALM 103:1

If God is not lost in our lives, if goodness is not lost in our lives, if memories are not lost in our lives, then we will have an easier time of finding our way to personal happiness. When I was a child, I lived according to a child's will: the need for love, the desire for warm days out back where the mock orange bushes grew. I lived to hear Johnny's voice call out from across the yard, inviting me to go turtle hunting.

If we are granted love at a young age, we are partially prepared for the journey. If we have known days of sudden glory packed with sucking icicles, rolling pumpkins down the farm road in October, playing Chutes and Ladders on the living room floor, anticipating the arrival of the grandparents with their luggage and lemon candies, then we are more exercised in human needs that will sustain us when we are in peril—and let us be reminded that we will all be placed in peril.

As I grew older, my mother and father and the cats and the house and my brothers and sisters began to fade into the past. It was then that I understood loneliness for the first time. I disliked school from the very beginning, but I had a place that was not confusing, frightening, dark, and that was in the house of my mother and father. But we have to leave the house of the father.

While it seemed that many of my classmates in high school were going somewhere with their lives, I felt that I was moved by default into a career, into a life that I did not choose. While I had attended college for a degree in education, and while I had taught high school English for over sixteen years, I knew all along that this was a diversion, or perhaps a link, or path, or ladder to help me along the way, for my way could not be planned.

Because I had taught high school English for all those years, I had to read American literature, British literature, plays, poems, great novels. By the forces of economy (I had a family and bills to sustain) I planned my lessons each day, drove to school, discussed literature with children, and regulated the checkbooks to balance the food, fuel, and clothing bills. Little did I know that during the habits of our being we accumulate interest in the account of the soul. That is where the journey lies. We can easily believe that our life's purpose is to accumulate wealth, develop a comfortable lifestyle, arrange our days into acceptable patterns that cause no pain. Such a life lived is a life sliding along the waxed mirror. Nothing stays, and we just see a reflection of the surface. It is the soul that breaks the mirror and pulls us into the substance.

I discovered this substance in my writing. The day's fruits are harvested many, many years later. Plant the seeds on rock, and the seeds blow away. Plant the seeds in sand, and they will not flourish. Plant the seeds in fertile soil, and there will be a harvest.

I did not know what the landscape under my feet held. I did not know my garden. I just read Shakespeare and Robert Frost and William Carlos Williams. I threw myself day after day into the early-morning rush hour to arrive at work on time, to do an honest day's labor with the children, to return to my house where Roe and the children waited to share with me the depths of their own plowing.

This afternoon as I write, I am listening to Maurice Ravel's "Pavane Pour Une Infante Defunte." It is a melancholy piece of music that helps me to sit back in my maple wood chair and remember. I remember carrying a bucket with the green turtle that Johnny and I caught in the swamp thirty years ago. The music helps me to remember how, when my sister was so angry that she had lost at Chutes and Ladders, she picked up the board and whacked it over my head. Ravel's music matches my memory of my grandmother and grandfather arriving from Belgium. The house was a new house when they arrived at the beginning of the summer. Ravel lifts a brown bag of lemon candies from under his vest and hands it to me, or is it the hand of my grandfather? The soul is reminded that icicles are meant to be snapped from the garage roof and eaten like ice cream by boys of eight as they trudge through the snow on their way to the lost past. When I listen to Ravel, I see a child pushing a pumpkin half his size down a dirt road toward his home because the local farmer said he could. The soul knows the feel of harvest soil.

Our poets and playwrights, our novelists and dreamers attempt to record the conventions of our lives as they adorn the soul's journey. We are not mere men and women in fur coats and brick houses but rather, extensions of love or potential love, carriers of a childhood, witnesses to a further range that waits for us as we collect what is eternal: the single passion, the useful call, the boiling certitude that wells up deep within our physical selves—the saved soul that has been promised to us.

Let us not be afraid or weary or lost as we wake up each morning. Let us not set the standards of our conquest to mean the maintenance of comfort but rather, the development of an inner presence: the lemon-candy memory, the turtle memory, the grandmother memory, the little memories that take hold of our being that prepares us for the coming of the Lord. Do not be afraid, for He is good.

In my passion, I find the risen Lord. In my loneliness, I find the risen Lord. In my weariness, I find the risen Lord. Praise God. Thank God. Be humble before the living God who has given us His only Son so that we may live with the knowledge of our own salvation. Sing praise to the risen Lord.

The Happiness of a Memory

When times are good, be happy.
ECCLESIASTES 7:14A

I met an old friend of mine at a wedding anniversary party. I hadn't seen John in over four years. As we stood next to each other and toasted the couple for continued success in their marriage, I casually asked John, "How is your old car doing?"

"The Model-A Ford?" John asked, just before he sipped his drink.

"Yes. I remember it was a green color? You keep it in your basement?"

"Oh, I'm thinking of selling it."

I nearly choked. "Sell it? Do you have a buyer?"

"A fellow who deals in antique cars said he'd like to buy it, but there hasn't been much action on his part. He hasn't even offered me a price."

"What condition is it in?" I watched Roe laughing with some friends across the room.

"I've had it in the heated garage for eight years. It has seventy-one thousand original miles on it. In eight years I drove it fifty miles."

I began to look at Roe more closely.

"Does it run?"

"Like a charm. About once a month I connect the battery, turn the key, and it starts right up."

"John, I'd be interested in looking at the car. Do you think the fellow you mentioned will buy it?"

"Don't know. As far as I'm concerned, it's on the market and first come, first served."

I walked between some people and around a chair, stood beside Roe, and began to laugh with the crowd, although I had no idea what they were laughing at. Roe turned to me and smiled. I smiled back.

In all good marriages there exists a shared decision-making agreement. Often this agreement is never discussed, it just evolves. The problem was that Roe and I never discussed how we would someday handle the decision to purchase a 1929 Model-A Ford.

First, let me explain why I wanted this car. When I was in high school, Jack Kruger, one of the most popular people in my senior class, drove to school one morning in a 1929 De Soto. He bought the car from a scrap heap, rebuilt the engine, and refinished the entire body of the car, both inside and out. I wanted to be like Jack Kruger when I was seventeen. What teenager wouldn't like to be popular?

One afternoon, the doorbell rang. I opened the door and there was Jack, Mr. Popular, on my porch, standing in my doorway. I didn't even think that Jack knew my name.

"Hi," he said. "I'm Jack Kruger. I think we're in the same class?"

"Yeah, hi," I said.

"My car died in front of your house, and I was wondering if I could leave it overnight in your driveway."

"Yeah, sure. My dad wouldn't mind."

"Could you help me push it? It's still in the road."

"Sure. Let me grab my shoes. I'll be right out." I ran to the kitchen, slipped on my pennyloafers, and joined Jack out on the driveway.

"I don't know what happened. It was working fine, when suddenly it coughed a bit, then died."

As we reached the end of the driveway, I turned and looked down the street: the 1929 De Soto. I didn't realize that he was talking about *the* car.

"I'll push from the driver's side and steer through the window. You push from the back."

Jack and I gave out a "One, two, three—push," and then the car slowly rolled forward.

"Great! Keep going," Jack called back.

I was pushing, I was touching Jack Kruger's 1929 De Soto!

By the time we pushed it far enough into the driveway, just under the red leaves of the Japanese maple, I was huffing and puffing.

"Thanks," Jack said. "Can I use your phone so my dad can pick me up?"

"That's okay. My dad will drive you home," which is what he did.

That night I walked out onto the driveway, stepped up to the De Soto, rubbed my hand against the side, and then I opened the driver's side door. I looked inside, smelled the old-car smell, and then I sat behind the wheel.

What seventeen-year-old kid wouldn't feel popular, handsome, smart, happy—sitting behind the wheel of a 1929 De Soto? I felt all those things that I was not when I was in high school.

The next morning a greasy, beat-up tow truck dragged the De Soto unceremoniously down the driveway and out onto the road. I never saw the car again, and I do not know what happened to it.

When Roe and I drove to John's house, I explained to her that he was seriously thinking about selling the car. "I just wanted to take a look." Roe smiled.

John met us in the driveway and directed me to park my car away from his garage door.

"Chris. Roe. Hello. Nice to see you."

"Nice to see you, too, John," I said as Roe and I walked up the driveway. As we approached the house, John pulled up the garage door, and there, sitting like a giant beetle with round, silver eyes, sat the 1929 Model-A Ford. It was light-olive green with black curves, chrome bumpers, a visor, luggage rack, runningboards—a jewel—a contraption—something that could be driven around the world. I admired the car as I admire antique furniture, old telephones and phonographs, and Victorian homes. I do not know anything about automobiles. My attraction to the Ford was purely for aesthetic reasons. I liked how it looked and, well, Jack Kruger had a 1929 De Soto, and look what it did for him!

As John opened the hood so I could admire the small engine, Roe smiled and shrugged her shoulders. Four weeks later, the Model-A rolled down the rear end of a flatbed truck and into my garage.

When everyone was in bed, I crept out the back door, slowly opened the garage door, and quickly slipped behind the wheel of the "A." Do you know what a forty-four-year-old man feels like, sitting behind the wheel of a 1929 Model-A Ford? Popular? Handsome? Smart? Happy? Nope—he just feels like a dumb, happy teenager.

We live our lives in a circle that seems to be rolling forward. If you feel old, or lost, or unhappy, renew your spirit by taking something from the past today and reliving the memory. You will discover that you really aren't lost or old, or unhappy. And remember, we are all rolling forward toward heaven.

Protect the child in me, Lord. Help me to laugh again. Teach me once again to see with the eyes of a child. I long to take delight in all that You have created. Protect me, Father. I am Your child. Protect me.

God Must Sometimes Think That We Are Funny People

How good and pleasant it is when brothers live together in unity!
PSALM 133:1

How is it that most of my near-death experiences involve my brother-in-law Peter? It was Peter and I who zoomed across a wide Canadian lake as a fierce thunderstorm tried to first electrocute us, then swallow us whole. It was Peter and I who barely escaped being run over by a boat during a midnight run along a river in fiberglass kayaks. And it was Peter and I who nearly blew up a car while we were in it.

I had to make one deal with Roe when I bought the 1929 Model-A Ford: She would not have to give up our single-car garage during the winter. Because I am long-gone in the early morning by the time she wakes up, and because she has to drive the three children to three separate schools, Roe felt it was too much to ask that her car be left out in the winter snow and ice while my Model-A slept peacefully in the dry garage from November to April. I also did not like the idea of Roe's scraping the ice from the windshield as the children waited in the kitchen to be driven to school.

Before I bought the car, I telephoned my brother-in-law.

"Hello, Peter. I did something."

"Hi, Chris. What's up?"

"Well, I did something that I can't exactly explain." I never took risks, never bought anything that was frivolous, and a 1929 Model-A Ford is, without a doubt, frivolous.

"What did you do?" Peter asked. Peter owns a bulldozer, a backhoe, an MGB, and a motorcycle. He flew helicopters and airplanes. He can fix the engine of a lawnmower and, probably, a Sherman tank.

"We-ell," I stammered. "I bought a 1929 Model-A Ford."

"Cool!" Peter said with great enthusiasm.

"I can't explain why I did it."

"You don't have to explain it to me," Peter reassured me. "I'm the one who bought a bulldozer for the fun of it, remember?"

"I was wondering if I could store it in one of your barns during the winter months? I don't want Roe to have to scrape snow and ice from the windshield in the middle of February."

Peter not only thought it was a great idea—he couldn't wait to drive it himself. He was also proud of me, Mr. Conservative, who doesn't like to drive fast, ski, or fly. I deeply dislike roller-coaster rides, and I faint at the sight of blood. No wonder Peter was startled that I had bought a dream machine, a Chitty-Chitty-Bang-Bang old-fashioned, clanking, jumping toy.

Last fall I drove the car to Peter's house, a fifty-mile drive along a major highway, down a few back roads, over a bridge, through a number of slow, twisting turns. After the long drive, at a steady forty-five miles per hour, I rolled down Peter's driveway and blew the horn. *Aooooogha!* Ah, the sound of folly.

Peter opened the passenger-side door, jumped in, and said, "Cool! Take me for a drive."

I spun around his driveway, made a left, and we were off. Moments later the car began to shake a bit, then wobble, cough, spit, misfire, backfire, cough some more, and then it rolled to a stop.

"I'll see what's the matter." Peter jumped from the car, walked to the front, and unlatched the hood. Flames shot out toward him like angry snakes. I jumped out of the car. The two of us began to dance around the burning engine.

"What do we do?" I yelled as Peter began blowing on the flames.

"Try to smother the flames." I picked up dirt and grass and threw it all on the engine. Nothing happened. After I began to blow on the flames also, I decided to I run to the backseat of the car. I grabbed a coat belonging to my son, rushed back to the burning engine, then I began to beat the flames with the coat. Still the fire burned and burned.

"Cut the gas supply, Chris! Cut the gas!" Peter yelled as he continued to frantically blow on the fire. As you may know, there was no such thing as fuel injection in 1929. The gas tank sits behind the engine just under the windshield, and gasoline is fed into the engine by gravity flow. Under the dashboard there is a small lever like a faucet that you have to turn on and off whenever you start or stop the car. This allows the gasoline into the engine. Cut the supply, and the car stops.

"Turn the gas off, Chris! The gas!"

I stumbled into the car as the flames grew and grew. I quickly turned the switch, and within seconds the fire stopped, for the gasoline flow was cut off and the remaining fuel burned away.

I had imagined the car's being engulfed in flames, the car's exploding, and the next day's headlines in the local paper: BROTHERS-IN-LAW FRIED: MODEL-A EXPLODES. WIVES ANGRY.

After the fire, Peter inspected the engine. Nothing was damaged, except my son's coat. There aren't any plastic parts in the Model-A engine. Things heated up a bit, but when all the metal parts cooled down after an hour, I turned the engine over. It caught and has been running fine ever since.

At the dinner table that night, as Peter described the flames to my sister, and I just gave a funny smile across the table to Roe, and as the children laughed, Peter turned to me and said—"Cool!"

When Jesus was asked what He hoped for His people, He answered that He hoped that we love each other. Invite a sister or brother today to join you on an adventure. Don't try setting your car on fire, but the two of you could gather wildflowers, or visit someone in the hospital, or paint the front door together. In our little acts of adventure we encounter with those we love, we please Jesus. Don't you think that God created the world for those who love?

In the embrace, we discover unity. In the word love, we discover God. Let us be united in love. Let us discover God together.

By Our Actions We Are Known
and Loved By God

Each one should test his own actions. Then he can take pride in himself, without comparing himself to somebody else, for each one should carry his own load.

GALATIANS 6:4–5

There was a grandfather clock in the house where I grew up. In my memory it stood ten feet high, leaned with a foreboding eye over anyone who passed, and ticked loudly. The clock had made its way from Belgium to our house during the voyage of 1948 when my parents and two brothers arrived in America on the *Queen Elizabeth*.

We retain memories that might not reflect the exact way things happened. I know that a pigeon visited our house for a few weeks, using the roof as a perch. I think I remember a tree that was struck by lightning. Perhaps hunters did not walk through our woods, carrying a dead deer. We have selective memories, a wide canvas with images that have been painted from one end to the other that is always in a state of flux.

I remember rolling marbles under the grandfather clock. I remember hiding Easter candy in the clock's belly. This clock's wood? Mahogany. The face? Brass. The numbers? Roman numerals. I do not remember hearing the chimes of the clock. Perhaps it had no chimes.

As the years moved through time, certain things in the house were rearranged: The kitchen table was turned to a new position; the living room table found its way against the wall. The grandfather clock was placed at the top of the stairs, just to the left of the first bedroom.

One afternoon, feeling productive, I decided to vacuum the living room and the dining room. As I made my way along the carpets, I turned into the front foyer. Then I decided that the stairs also needed to be cleaned. I slowly made my way up each step. Back and forth, back and forth. The vacuum whirred. As I reached the top of the stairs, I had to decide if I would continue cleaning the upstairs bedrooms. I looked around, checked the rooms, looked at the carpets. They all needed a good cleaning, so I returned to the vacuum cleaner and continued on my way.

I found myself standing before the grandfather clock, the tall, the wise, the stern grandfather clock. I kneeled, bent over, and checked around to see if there was much dust under the clock. There was.

As the vacuum cleaner continued to inhale and roar, I reached around the waist of the clock. It was my intention to tip the clock forward a bit so that I could clean underneath.

With the vacuum hose in my left hand and my left cheek pressed against the clock, I slowly pulled the timepiece forward with my right arm. Suddenly a tremendous *crash!* dominated the sound of the vacuum cleaner, exploding throughout the house. I looked over my shoulder as the top half of the clock banged, bounced, rolled, rumbled, smashed down and down and down the stairs until it landed in the foyer below. Gears, wire, wood all crumbled into an unrecognizable mess of destruction.

My mother ran out from the kitchen. My father ran out from his study. My sisters and brothers appeared from all directions. There I stood with the bottom half of the grandfather clock still in my arms. They all looked at me. "Oops!"

"Christopher? What happened?" my mother asked as she shut off the vacuum.

"I don't know."

"Are you hurt?" my father asked as he picked up a some wires and gears from the broken clock.

"No, Dad. I'm okay."

"Boy, are you gonna get it," my sister cackled with delight.

How was I to know that the grandfather clock was built in two pieces—the base and the clockworks? The clock itself was simply resting on top of the main casing. When I leaned the clock forward to clean under it, the top part tipped, flew over my head, and crashed down the entire flight of stairs.

"You are lucky that you weren't hurt," my mother said as she pushed the clock back against the wall.

"Too bad," my sister laughed.

"Hey, at least I was trying to clean up around here!" I yelled.

For days afterward I felt guilty that I had decapitated my parents' grandfather clock. A few months later my father carried the base of the clock into the attic, and there it stayed.

A few weeks ago during a quick visit to my parents' house, my mother asked if I would carry some boxes to the attic. When I opened the attic door, I placed a box to my right, then I looked up. There, leaning over me, stood the grandfather clock's casing, still headless. I realized that the clock had never stood ten feet tall and had never scowled an evil eye.

Perhaps most of our childhood memories are just distortions, illusions, myths we create in our minds to simply explain away those many years spent back when we didn't know very much and didn't care.

Just before I stepped from the attic, I gave what was left of the grandfather clock a final inspection. Then I noticed that the door of the clock was loose. I walked up, pulled back the door, and found, still wrapped in yellow cellophane, a sugar Easter egg with a small inscription written with frosting: EASTER *1961*.

We discover proof of our own existence in the most unlikely places. I *was* ten years old once, and I really *did* hide Easter candy in the belly of the clock.

Each day we seek proof that we are of value in our world. By the acts of kindness, we are seen by God. By our acts of gratitude, we are seen by God. By our acts of charity, we are seen by God. Therein lies our value.

I believe in myself. I believe in my worthiness. I believe in my abilities. I believe in my strength. I believe in my goodness. Thank You, Lord Jesus, for believing in me.

Daughters of God the Father

The daughters of men were beautiful.

GENESIS 6:2

Daughters. What to do about daughters? Plant a radish, and you get a radish. But plant a daughter, and she turns into a woman!

I held Karen the day she was born. I looked into her small eyes. Yes, she looked like a girl. She wiggled a bit, cooed, held my finger, spit up.

When Karen was two, she didn't like the feel of grass on her legs. When she was eight, she liked the swing, the cat, her blanket. She ate like a girl, giggled like a girl, slept with her doll under her arms, and she liked how her bangs didn't fall into her eyes.

Something happened. I knew that Karen had turned twelve, but there was something more.

Was it a change in the atmospheric pressure? Was there something in the water? Had I missed something?

I was sitting recently at the edge of Karen's bed just before she clicked off her table lamp. We are in the habit of talking before she sleeps.

"Daddy. I'm so excited. Tomorrow the whole class is going to Medieval Times. I can't wait."

Medieval Times is a local restaurant, an entertainment extravaganza where people dress up as kings, queens, and knights preparing for battle. As the audience cheers and eats, they watch actual jousting competitions with live horses and men in real suits of armor.

"Daddy, I heard that at the end of the competition, the winning knight walks around the arena with a basket of roses. He takes one rose out at a time, kisses it, then throws it into the audience."

I looked down at Karen as she spoke. She no longer has bangs, and I could not remember the last time I pushed her on a swing.

"Daddy, I'm so excited. I think tomorrow will be my lucky day, and I will catch a rose from the knight."

"Now, Karen don't get your hopes up. There are hundreds of people in the audience and I don't think the knight has that many roses."

"Tomorrow's my lucky day," Karen whispered as she kissed me good-night, arranged her pillow, and turned off her light.

Since when did Karen give up her Cinderella sheets and pillowcase? I wondered as I kissed her good-night and slowly walked out of her room.

"Good-night, Daddy."

"Good-night, my girl."

The next day on my way to work, as is my habit, I stopped in town at the milk store to buy the newspaper. As I stood in line, I noticed on the counter a small sign: SILK ROSES. Sitting behind the sign were fifteen or twenty tiny silk roses wrapped in rolled cellophane.

"How much are the roses?" I asked the cashier.

"A dollar."

I picked a rose, slipped it into my pocket, paid for the paper and the flower, and then I drove to work.

That night at the dinner table I asked the family about their day. David received a 97 on his biology test. Michael lost his two-headed nickel that I gave him for his birthday, and Karen loved Medieval Times.

"It was great!" Karen nearly sang with glee. "The horses ran real fast. We were rooting for the Green Knight. He won. I didn't like the dessert, but the Queen was pretty. I loved it."

"Did you catch a rose, Karen?" I didn't want to ask.

"No," she said softly. She looked down into her dinner plate, but then she perked up with renewed excitement. "We could drink all the soda we wanted, and the flags were purple and yellow. We got to wear paper crowns and drink from frosted mugs. Just like in the old times."

Later that night, when it was time for bed, I carried Michael on my back. "Can we go to Medieval Times someday?" he asked.

"Sure. You can be a knight in shining armor."

"I want a frosted mug," Michael said as I tucked him into bed.

By the time I entered Karen's room, she was already under her covers. "Daddy, I had fun today."

"I'm so glad." I reached into my suit pocket and pulled out the single silk rose.

Karen looked at me with her beautiful round eyes. As she smiled, her braces gleamed between her lips. "Thank you, Daddy!"

"I thought you might like this."

"I knew today would be my lucky day," she said as she hugged me.

"You're welcome, my young woman." I kissed her good-night as she placed the rose on her pillow.

"Good-night, Daddy. I love you."

"I love you too."

I think a father's job is to be with his children at just the right time with just the right rose.

My rose, my daughter, my Karen. May she always remember her father as the brave, good knight.

God knew what He was doing when He created daughters. Today would be a good day to write your daughter a letter, or give her a phone call for no other reason than to just say "Hello. I love you."

For the brush on the sink, I thank You, Lord. For the picture in the frame, I praise You. For the voice on the phone, I thank You, Lord. For the hug from this girl, I praise You. Dear Lord, thank You and thank You for daughters. Yes, thank heaven for little girls.

Money Well-Spent

Jesus answered, "If you want to be perfect, go, sell your possessions and give to the poor, and you will have treasure in heaven. Then come, follow me."

MATTHEW 19:21

A long, long time ago when lilacs were purple and the fence was green, my sister Anne and I decided to be entrepreneurs.

When we were children, we were given a quarter as an allowance once a week and anything we could find between the couch pillows and in our father's suit jackets.

A quarter was a great deal of money in 1959 for an eight-year-old boy. Cracker Jacks, Ring-Dings, Kraft Marshmallows, a box of brown pretzels, Bonomo's Turkish Taffy, a Superman comic book, all a quarter a piece. What boy didn't feel wealthy walking into the 5 & 10 on a Saturday morning with a quarter in his pocket?

At some point, Anne and I realized that two quarters were better than one, and a dollar was gold.

When she and I announced at the dinner table one evening that we wanted to earn some money, my mother smiled, saying that we had all we needed. My father looked us over, probably appraising our resolve, then he suggested that we try to sell watercress at the side of the road.

Watercress. I thought only my family and ducks knew of its existence. I always associated watercress with ducks because my father first discovered wild watercress in the swamp out back where the mallards squawked in the summer and children squawked in the winter as we skated back and forth arm in arm, or chased the girls or were chased by the girls.

Papa convinced Anne and me there was a market for watercress, so she and I set out the next day to construct our watercress stand.

During those green and yellow days my father was in the publishing business and often had books delivered to the house in large wood crates. He stored the empty crates in the garage just in case someday, someone might want to build a watercress stand.

Anne and I rolled the wheelbarrow into the garage. The garage housed the sailboat that my father had built, old storm windows, newspapers, screens, and a tobacco pipe. (I once found a pipe behind the storm windows that had never been used. My father didn't smoke. I thought it was such a forbidden object that I smelled the tobacco residue, held the pipe in my hand, and then I pushed it back behind the storm windows. Perhaps the pipe is still there today.)

My sister and I tipped two of the heavy crates onto the wheelbarrow and pushed the load down the long driveway until we reached the front hedge. We spun around to the front of the hedge and dumped the crates onto the sidewalk.

"Let's stand them on their sides. We can find a board and place that on top of the boxes. That way we'll have a counter to set up the watercress," Anne suggested.

We ran back into the garage, found the exact board we needed, returned to the road, and assembled our little store. Now that I look back, I realize that most of the fun of being a child is in the construction of the idea and not in the final implementation.

Papa suggested that we fill pickle bottles with water, then place clumps of watercress in each bottle. "That way, people will see that your product is still fresh."

My grandmother liked to keep every bottle that ever entered the house, so it was an easy task to find six or seven pickle jars. While Anne carried the jars to our stand, I ran down the back lawn to the small pond where my father cultivated strands of the wild watercress. Much of a child's life ought to involve running down a wide, green lawn to the bottom of the hill to where the pond spreads out like an invitation on a table.

I remember kneeling on a rock at the lip of the pond. I reached out, plunged my skinny arm into the cool water, opened my fingers, and grabbed a clump of watercress. I liked the tickling feeling of the green vegetation against my small palm. By the time I was finished, I had harvested all the watercress that was in the pond. I hadn't brought a bucket, so I scooped up all the watercress into my arms, pressing it against my chest, and then I ran back up the hill to the front of the yard, where Anne was already painting the last letters to our sign: FRESH WATERCRESS—50¢ A BUNCH.

"What are you gonna do with your money?" I asked Anne as she tried to clean the paintbrush against the grass.

"I don't know. I was thinking about giving it to the poor."

"What?"

"The poor. I was thinking about giving it to the poor. You know, poor people?"

I didn't know any poor people, but I remembered the brass box built into the back wall of the church with the brass letters embossed in a plaque: POOR BOX.

Anne and I nailed two broomsticks to both sides of our watercress stand, then we nailed our sign from one end to the other. After we dragged lawn chairs out to the road, we sat down and waited for our millions.

One car rushed along the road. Two cars. Ten cars. Fifty cars. We began to play a game. Anne would take the cars that zoomed down from the left, and I would take the cars that zoomed from the right, and we would see who accumulated the first hundred white cars. Anne won.

As the afternoon sun curved down toward the west, Anne and I eventually abandoned our business. We dismantled the stand, carried the crates back to the garage, and delivered our unsold supply to my mother.

That night, after a full meal of stew, French fries, and bowls and bowls of watercress, my father asked how we had done.

"Didn't sell a nickel," Anne shrugged.

I looked into her eyes. I could not understand why she looked so disappointed.

"What's the matter, Anne?" my father asked.

"Well, some kid is going to be hungry tomorrow."

"What's that?" my mother said as she brushed the hair from my sister's eyes.

"I read that a quarter can feed a poor kid for a day. I read that in one of those *Maryknoll* magazines."

"What's Maryknoll?" I asked.

"I don't know. Just a magazine Mom has. It's full of pictures of kids like us."

After dinner, Anne and I retreated to the living room. As we sat on the couch, she repeated, "Some kid is going to be hungry tomorrow."

During a commercial, I had to run upstairs to the bathroom. As I was walking back down the stairs, I noticed that my father was standing beside the closet beside the front door. I stopped, sat on the dark stairs, and watched him.

He pulled out a handful of coins from a box and began placing them into every pocket of all his suits. *So that is why there is money in his pockets,* I thought.

After the television program was over, I suggested to Anne that we go see if there was any change in Papa's pockets. She and I ran to the closet and, when we made our final count, discovered over four dollars in coins.

That Sunday, after church, Anne and I took turns dropping the quarters, dimes, and nickels into the brass poor box. *Clink. Clink. Clink.*

We, as people of God, have an obligation to help the poor. Such help can be in a prayer said each day, in a donation to a favorite charity, in a small gift sent to a neighbor in need. Charity begins in the home.

I am rich in prayer. I am rich in love. I am rich in my faith. Guide me, Lord, in how I can best share my wealth.

The Way, the Truth, and the Light

Have faith in God.

MARK 11:22

I am asked to speak at various functions during the year about books and writing. After I read a few excerpts from my work, I often leave some time for people to ask questions. This is an excerpt from a recording during one of those after-talk interviews.

Question: *Mr. de Vinck. How did you become a writer?*

Answer: My mother and father were both writers—my mother a poet and my father a philosopher. I didn't become a writer because of their influence as writers. I became a writer partly because of their influence as parents who provided me with five brothers and sisters, a big old house, woods, swamps, security. I have lived all my adult life with a deep sense of longing, and part of that longing is a dream to walk back down the driveway of my home where my father might be still washing the car and my mother is out on the lawn, reading the newspaper, and I have a full afternoon waiting for me where my brothers have raked a path in the woods and they have invited me to Sherwood Forest if I can find a sword and a rope.

Question: *So would you say your inspiration comes from your childhood?*

Answer: I wouldn't call it "inspiration." We develop into people who have strengths and weaknesses. One of my weaknesses is not

182

wanting to let go of anything. I also am cursed, perhaps, with a very good memory, not school-related memory for dates and formulas but rather, for personal memories. I tend to keep everything. I suppose my mind is cluttered. I try to arrange some sort of order to my life, an order that is imposed on me.

Question: *How can order be imposed upon your memories?*

Answer: There seems to be a driving force in all of us that helps the mind endure what is sometimes unendurable. How is it that people who are very old do not run through the streets, mad with fear that they will die in a week or in a year? The human mind has some sort of ability to adjust itself. I think that is God's doing. He does not want us to be afraid.

Question: *Does God play a role in the creative powers?*

Answer: If there is no God, there is not art.

Question: *Do you think Mozart was concerned about God?*

Answer: I do not know Mozart's biography, but I know God's biography, and it is written that God is in everything we do. God was very concerned about Mozart. Can you imagine the burden of being one of God's messengers? Who could write music like Mozart's if it were not for the hand of God?

Question: *So artists have an exclusive, direct pipeline to God's instructions?*

Answer: Oh, of course not, not artists alone. Everyone. We all have God nudging us. Some people live quiet lives, being famous in their homes, creating the art of living. Such people are under God's influence just as much as Mozart, or Copland, or Dickinson, or Morrison.

Question: *Let me return to my original question, then. How did you become a writer?*

Answer: Well, my parents, especially my mother, provided the model for seeing. She saw things that I would have never seen, and she was a good teacher. She pointed to ferns, colors, leaves in the yard, funny jokes and stories in magazines. When my mother came upon something that delighted her, she would share it with the family, and then it would be ours too.

Question: *We've read that you began to write when you were twenty-three years old.*

Answer: Yes. That's correct. I was a graduate student in Teachers College, Columbia University.

Question: *In New York City?*

Answer: Yes, New York. I lived in a graduate dorm. My room overlooked the alley where the garbage trucks would grind and crush the trash at 5:30 each Saturday morning.

Question: *How is it that you know the exact year that you began to write? Did you have something published that year?*

Answer: Oh, no. I wasn't published until ten years after I began my writing. I can even tell you the month I began to write: January 1974. I was terribly lonely during that time of my life. A young woman I thought I loved didn't fall in love with me. We broke off our relationship. My neighbor in the room next door was making love to his girlfriend every other night, it seemed to me. I was reading William Carlos Williams at the time.

Question: *What would you compare the creative process to?*

Answer: Faith.

Question: *How so?*

Answer: We believe in God. I believe in God. My mother taught me about His existence. I do not see God, but I believe He exists. At times I have grave doubts, believe there is nothing after death but dust and oblivion, but then, like a man who wipes his brow after a long day of plowing, I return to the belief that there will be a crop to harvest. Writing, for me, is like a cycle that wavers between doubt and certitude. When I finish an essay or poem that pleases me, I often thank God, deeply thank God for the creation of the newest piece. But then I go through a few days when I doubt that the essay or poem is very good. I doubt that I will be able to continue with the writing, that I will ever produce something of lasting worth and beauty, but then I wipe my brow and return to my faith, and that faith tells me that my work will not abandon me, that God will not abandon me, that I can, indeed continue with my plowing for the harvest festival.

Let us lock arms at the field's edge and dance the harvest dance in celebration of God: the blood of life, the air we breathe, the salt in the sea. God, my God, have mercy on us.

The Words of God

The words of the LORD are flawless, like silver refined in a furnace of clay, purified seven times.

PSALM 12:6

Most nights I read aloud to my children before they sleep: *Mr. Popper's Penguins, My Father's Dragon, Treasure Island, James and the Giant Peach,* the rhymes of Mother Goose, and the Bible. I have been doing this for the past thirteen years. Lately I've been trying to figure out if it has been worth the effort.

Oh, I believe the psychologist Jean Piaget when he speaks about assimilation—children picking up information that fits in with what they already know. My children have heard thousands of different sentence patterns repeated over and over again as they sat beside me during those many nights of the four seasons.

To be sure, my children have picked up new words along the way. When my oldest son, David, was four years old, he walked around the house, stating that he felt *soporific* after he heard about the "soporific effects" that lettuce had on Beatrix Potter's slothful rabbits. Karen learned what a *bungalow* was as she listened how Uncle Wiggley crawled out from his home at the beginning of each new adventure.

Of course, it is true that a rich reading background adds to, what I call, a child's intellectual baggage. I have been an English teacher for the past sixteen years and I have had, for the most part, two types of students: those who have a rich personal background and those who have this personal experience *and* a wide reading experience.

All children come to schools with a wide diversity of personal experiences. I would say of those children that only ten percent also come with a wide reading background. The child with the widest personal *and* widest reading background seems to be carrying the most intellectual baggage into my classroom year after year. This is the child who, eventually, scores the highest on the verbal section of the S.A.T., who is able to make sudden and clear connections between books and life, who has the strongest sense of what it means to live a life of reflection, who is the stronger writer. The S.A.T. *is* a very biased test. It is biased against those who do not read.

Thinking is looking at experiences and making conclusions. Writing is the physical evidence of our thinking. The more we experience, the more information we have inside our minds and hearts. The more information we have, the better conclusions we can make about our own lives.

Nevertheless, I read aloud to my children each night for reasons that go beyond Piaget, vocabulary, writing, and information retrieval.

I want eight-year-old Michael to taste the chocolate as Willie Wonka guides the children on a grand tour of his factory. I want Karen to smell the flowers that Francie Nolan's father bought for her in *A Tree Grows in Brooklyn*. I want my children to feel the hunger that Richard Wright endured in *Black Boy*. I want my son David, someday, to smack his hand against Boo Radley's house in *To Kill a Mockingbird*. I want my daughter to feel the moonlight against her bare breasts as did Annie in Jamaica Kincaid's glorious little book *Annie John*.

I read aloud to my children because I want them to feel the hand of Ivan Illyich against their cheek just before he dies. I want my children to someday receive the blessing of Father Zossima in *Brothers Karamazov*. I want my children to believe that it can, indeed, rain flowers as it did in *One Hundred Years of Solitude*. I want my children to watch Sydney Carton walk up the steps to the guillotine. I want them to carry Addie's coffin along with Faulkner in *As I Lay Dying*. I want my children to listen to Reb Saunders in *The Chosen*. I want the water from the pump in *The Miracle Worker* to run against the small hands of David, Karen, and Michael.

"Mrs. Keller!" Annie Sullivan screams out with joy to Helen's mother, "Mrs. Keller! Mrs. Keller! She knows!" Helen Keller finally learned that these funny little symbols, *a-b-c-d*, mean words, sentences, language, life, freedom. "She knows!"

Reading makes possible the connection between our minds and our near-magical notions drawn up from our impossible hearts. I also read to my children because I like the feel of their warmth against my arms and the sound of their quiet breath as they listen to my voice circling around them night after night.

Reading aloud to children every day gives them the widest entry to that place we call freedom. Reading aloud to children begins the slow process of education that ends in parents and teachers celebrating, with joy—"They know! They know! Their hearts and minds have made the connections. Our children are free. They know!"

Perhaps you can buy a Bible for your children today. Perhaps you can take ten minutes each evening, beginning tonight, and start reading aloud: *"In the beginning God created the heavens and the earth. Now the earth was formless and empty, darkness was over the* surface of the deep, and the Spirit of God was hovering over the waters. And God said, 'Let there be light'" (Genesis 1:1–3).

The words in the Bible, the words, the words, are the words of God, such words whispered in the evening, such words stretched out along the wide lands, the words in the corner of the poorest home, the words of God. How filled with gratitude we are for the words, the words, the words.

Epilogue

On the last and greatest day of the Feast, Jesus stood and said in a loud voice, "If a man is thirsty, let him come to me and drink. Whoever believes in me, as the Scripture has said, streams of living water will flow from within him."

JOHN 7:37–38

Acknowledgments

"Words of God" originally appeared in *The Wall Street Journal,*
November 22, 1992. Copyright © 1992 Dow Jones & Company
Princeton, New Jersey.

"May God Protect Us and Forgive Us" originally appeared in *The
Evangelist,* July 29, 1993, Albany, N.Y.

"Inside Goodness" originally appeared in *Daily Guideposts,* 1991.
Copyright © 1990 by Guideposts, Carmel, N.Y. 10512.

A portion of "God and Suffering" originally appeared in *Daily
Guideposts,* 1995. Copyright © 1994 by Guideposts, Carmel,
N.Y. 10512.

A portion of "Pointing to the Promised Land" originally appeared in
Daily Guideposts, 1992. Copyright © 1991 by Guideposts,
Carmel, N.Y. 10512.